Flak Jacket and Lipstick

Alistair W. Taylor

Alan. Witcutt.

CHRISTINE
WITCUTT

Flak Jacket and Lipstick

The Life of Christine Witcutt

Alistair W Taylor and Alan Witcutt

THE MERCAT PRESS
EDINBURGH

First published in 1994 by Mercat Press
James Thin, 53 South Bridge, Edinburgh EH1 1YS

ISBN 1873644 272

Set in Plantin 10/12 point from author generated discs by
City Litho Company
Printed and bound in Great Britain by
Biddles Ltd, Guildford and King's Lynn

Contents

Illustrations

Maps

Acknowledgements

This book is very much a family effort. It might never have been written without the motivation given by Christine's niece, Alison Taylor, who transcribed hundreds of pages of Christine's diaries and journals, reviewed and edited the drafts and encouraged her father Alistair, Christine Witcutt's brother. Christine's husband, Alan, was the co-author. The maps were drawn by her daughter, Julie, while her son, Paul, recorded the interviews with Edinburgh Direct Aid volunteers on which Chapter 9 is based. Elspeth Thorburn, Christine's sister, made the initial contact with Mercat Press, and coordinated the selection of the photographs which illustrate the book. Joan Lee, Alistair's wife, also helped to review and edit the drafts. Jessie Taylor, Christine's mother, gave permission to use the letter that appears in Chapter 8.

Many other people made important contributions to the publication of this book. Ian McHaffie suggested offering the manuscript to Mercat Press. Lucy McHaffie photocopied several hundred pages of journals and diaries. Don Crowson reviewed several draft chapters and offered valuable editorial comment. Janice Wald and Karen Simmons helped out with the typing when deadlines were pressing, and also reviewed some of the draft material. The Rev. Andrew McLellan, Minister of St Andrews and St George's Church in Edinburgh, graciously allowed us to use his text for the BBC 2 programme, 'Pause for Thought', which captured so well what it was like for Alan when he returned in a state of shock from Sarajevo.

Christine's diaries alone could not tell the complete story of her two trips to Bosnia. The authors are indebted to Denis Rutovitz, whose diaries and records of EDA's convoys to Croatia and Bosnia have been used extensively to corroborate statements in Christine's diaries and to fill in details missing from her written record. Above all, the authors wish to thank Brian Horne, whose acute journalist's vision, insight and recollections, captured in tape-recorded interviews, enabled them to complete the story of the second, fatal trip to Bosnia, particularly the last four days, when Christine had no opportunity to write in her diary.

Brian and Denis have both written moving tributes to Christine which appear, respectively, in the Introduction and Chapter 10. Denis's account of the founding of Edinburgh Direct Aid, quoted in Chapter 6, speaks for all aid workers who risk their lives to bring help to the victims of war and atrocity.

Finally, we would like to express our appreciation to Seán Costello and Tom Johnstone of Mercat Press, without whose interest and encouragement this book would never have made it into print.

Glossary of Terms and Abbreviations

The 'Halley':	a Renault 17 ton removal van, originally owned by Halley Transport and loaned to EDA. Also referred to as the 'Renault'. EDA later purchased the Halley.
The 'Bumble':	an ex-army Bedford MK 7.5/10 ton truck, painted yellow and black, owned by Chris Chapman, an EDA volunteer.
The 'Hippo' or 'TL':	a Bedford TL 7.5 ton truck owned by EDA.

T2; Laufzettel:	documents needed in order to cross borders with trucks.
Četniks:	Serbian royalist guerrillas, formed as a resistance movement to fight the Germans and Italians after the Nazi invasion of Yugoslavia during WW II. Later fought the Croatian Ustaše and the Communist Partisans during the civil war which followed . Pronounced 'Chetniks'.
Partisans:	Communist resistance fighters led by Tito, who fought the Germans and Italians during WW II, but were more concerned with eliminating the Četniks in the civil war.
Ustaše:	Croatian fascist extremists who collaborated with Hitler and Mussolini and conducted a genocidal campaign against the Serbian minorities of Croatia and Bosnia during WW II. Pronounced 'Ustashay'.
BDA:	Bosnian Disaster Appeal
EDA:	Edinburgh Direct Aid to Bosnia-Herzegovina and Croatia
HVO:	Croatian Militia and/or Army.
ICRC:	International Committee of the Red Cross
IRC:	International Refugee Council
JNA:	Yugoslav People's Army.
MAM:	WW2 US Army trucks
SEA:	Scottish European Aid
UNHCR:	United Nations High Commission on Refugees
UNPROFOR:	United Nations Protection Force
WHO:	World Health Organization

Guide to Pronunciation

One of the decisions which has to be made when writing a book of this type is whether to anglicise the spelling of foreign words and names. The authors have chosen to use Serbo-Croatian spelling in general, which demands a key to the correct pronunciation of unfamiliar letters. The authors have made every effort to ensure that the names of persons and places have been accurately spelled, and apologise for any errors.

The pronunciation of Latin letters with the various modifiers found in Serbo-Croatian is approximately as indicated in the following table, where the words to the right are to be given their typical English sound values. The other letters not listed here are pronounced much as they are in English.

c	'ts' as in 'rats'
č	'ch' as in 'charcoal'
ć	't' as in 'picture'
dj	'j' as in 'jug'
dž	'j' as in 'jack'
i	'i' as in 'machine'
j	'y' as in 'yet'
lj	'lli' as in 'million'
nj	'ni' as in 'onion'
š	'sh' as in 'shell'
u	'u' as in 'rule'
z	'z' as in 'zebra'
ž	's' as in 'pleasure'

Introduction

Homeward bound at last, the little convoy of trucks wound its way slowly through the rubble-filled streets of Sarajevo. After many setbacks and near-disasters, several tons of food and other essential supplies had been delivered to the enemy-encircled city. The volunteers were tired, but happy that their job was done. They began to think about the hot baths and clean clothes waiting for them back home in Edinburgh.

On the shattered motorway leading to the airport, known around the world as 'Snipers' Alley', a single bullet ricocheted off the windshield pillar of the second truck. Christine Witcutt slumped forward, unconscious and bleeding. Two CNN reporters rushed her to a United Nations army hospital. French surgeons tried desperately to save her life, but to no avail.

In writing this account of Christine's life, the tragic realities of her death and the horror of the war in Bosnia were often overwhelming. But this story is not about death and despair. It is about life and joy, passion and commitment, courage and caring.

Christine was never more alive than during those last two weeks. She believed whole-heartedly in what she was doing – that her efforts could make a difference. She was exhilarated by the thrill of danger and revelled in her ability to meet every challenge. Brian Horne, a journalist who was sitting next to Christine when the sniper's bullet struck, captured something of her exuberance and inner strength when he wrote:

Add a (temporarily lapsed) vegetarian feminist to a bunch of odd bods driving trucks through Bosnia and what do you get? Mugs of tea and cheese rolls, thank goodness! Mere principles didn't stop Christine playing Mum and rustling up a quick snack for the lads at some of the inevitable halts along the road. Or tucking into tins of stew at the end of a long day as though lentils had never been discovered.

Oh well, Bosnia is the sort of place where it's impossible to get along without the odd little compromise here and there. But some standards were never allowed to slip.

Picture the scene. Things are getting a bit dodgy and everyone else is adjusting helmet straps or tugging at flak jackets. Meanwhile, Christine whips out her lipstick. Putting a brave face on it, you might say.

Degrees of danger can only be just a guess for the inexperienced. But when the first words heard after your ears stop ringing from the crash of a mortar is one of Her Majesty's finest telling his officer in charge: 'That last impact was a bit close, sir!' then possibly a little hint of worry might be in order?

Wrong! Christine's face showed only a radiant smile of self-confidence. There had been times in the past when it had been hinted she might not be able to take such pressure. Now Christine knew she could.

It had been a long, hard day, travelling in the mountains with British troops from the UN base at Vitez in Central Bosnia. We were investigating stories of atrocities, of murdered children, but no evidence was found that day. In a village nearby, however, a young woman had been driven by hunger, desperation and who knows what else to hang herself.

Feelings were running high and likely to be relieved by loosing off a few rounds, just for the hell of it, at any likely target. The trouble really started when fighting erupted round a strategic crossroads on the way back to base. Muslims on one side, Croats on the other and a small contingent of Edinburgh Direct Aid in the middle, thankful for a British Army escort.

We crouched behind their Land Rovers for about as long as it takes six thirsty people with very dry mouths to share a can of warm Coca Cola, wondering what the next move would be and eyeing up a nearby deep ditch. Never have nettles looked so attractive and inviting. But the order came to move out – fast. Speeding down the road, that mortar was a last, loud reminder of the uncomfortable situation left behind. Stupid perhaps, but once the pressure was off and the danger had passed, we were as high as kites. 'And they said I would be the first to crack,' smirked Christine.

That look of triumph is something to be remembered. Just like the voice organising inter-truck sing-song competitions – a shocking misuse of the CB radios, but it helped eat up the long miles. It takes a school teacher to do something like that.

When two vehicles were smashed after a bad skid on a wet, greasy road outside the Adriatic port of Split, all that practice gained dabbing scraped knees in school playgrounds came in handy as Christine applied dressings to bleeding heads.

No Christine, you didn't crack. Not in Sarajevo, sheltering in the early morning as shells filled the air with screaming shards of metal and brought death and terror to a market-place only thirty metres away. Not even on that sunny July afternoon when ,nevous, excited, elated, we headed home. Like the rest, your eyes were fixed on the road ahead, keeping a look-out for the most obvious danger – pot holes.

You didn't crack in that awful moment in the cab when a shattering blow, like a hammer striking metal, gave way to an unbelievable stillness and silence. You didn't move, you didn't flinch, you didn't scream. Not a sound.

Don't worry, Christine, the rest of us will do the shouting for you.

Christine's death was headline news all over Britain. Reporters for a Scottish newspaper soon discovered that she had kept a diary of her two relief trips to Bosnia. Their interest in the diaries was the inspiration for this book.

The idea of reading someone else's diary has a certain fascination for most of us. Christine's journals were not secret, but they were private. She started them when she was seventeen, set them aside when marriage, work and children consumed all her time, and returned to writing after her early retirement. Well-written, with a wry and self-deprecating humour, they give us two windows into her life and spirit, one tinted by the optimism and insecurity of youth, the other tempered by the wisdom and disillusionment of maturity. Both show us a strong, intelligent, thoughtful and active woman, who loved literature, poetry, music and the remote beauties of the Scottish Highlands.

Using her own words wherever possible, this book tells the story of Christine's life, from her birth during the Clydebank Blitz, through school, a teaching career, courtship, marriage and children, to her retirement in 1992. It traces her long association with Yugoslavia, from her first holiday trip in 1963 to the fatal Sarajevo expedition.

The diaries of her two trips to Bosnia with Edinburgh Direct Aid are printed in full, letting us share the excitement, the frustration and the random horror of life today in what was once a holiday paradise. We enjoy happy hours with refugees, villagers, children, soldiers of the United Nations Protection Force and other aid workers, and share the hospitality of the citizens of beleaguered Sarajevo. We live through moments of gut-wrenching tension at checkpoints, confronted by hostile armed militiamen. We watch helplessly as the Bosnian-Serb besiegers tear open half the boxes in the lead truck, shouting that only food is humanitarian aid, and seize all the drugs and other medical supplies intended for the hospital in Sarajevo. Through all of this, we sense Christine's joy in the beauty of Yugoslavia's scenery and her compassion for the tragic lot of its people.

What was it in Christine's nature, upbringing and experience that drove her to risk and lose her life in the horrors of Yugoslavia's civil war? What caused the war and how can it be ended? What evil can drive civilised human beings, who lived together for so many years in apparent harmony, to perpetrate such hideous atrocities on their former friends and neighbours? If this book can shed some light on these questions for the reader, the authors will rest satisfied.

1

Childhood Influences

In the Spring of 1941, the German Luftwaffe mounted a deadly bombing campaign against the Glasgow shipyards, later to be known as the 'Clydebank Blitz'. Careless marking by the lead aircraft resulted in heavy bombing of the housing districts of Clydebank, killing nearly 2,000 people and injuring many more. In the midst of this holocaust, Jessie Taylor, a housewife living in the suburban town of Clarkston, south of the Clyde in the County of Renfrewshire, gave birth to a daughter who was named Christine, after Jessie's mother and her husband's sister. Jessie, who had all three of her children at home, remembers that it was impossible to get a doctor to attend the birth, because every available physician was working round the clock to treat the victims of the German air raids. Christine was the second of three children. Her brother, Alistair, was nearly three years old when Christine was born, while Elspeth did not appear on the scene until Christine was six.

Christine's father, James Brown Taylor, known to everyone as Jim, was a journeyman electrician with the Emergency Section of the Glasgow Corporation Electricity Department. In wartime, the work of restoring electrical service to industrial premises and homes is of national importance, so Jim was exempted from military service. When his shift work permitted, he also acted as a volunteer fire warden. As a result, his family saw little of him during the war years. Yet his was surely the strongest single influence on the values and characters of his children.

Jim was born in 1903, in the working class district of Springburn. Jim's father, who worked in the railway engine shops of Glasgow's North British Locomotive Works (now long-defunct), was blacklisted for trade union activities and had to leave Britain before the First World War to find employment. After some time in Canada, he ended up in South Africa for the duration of the war. For several years, his family received no word from him and did not know if he was alive or dead. As a result, Jim left school at fourteen in order to support his mother, brother and sisters. This willingness to sacrifice his own interests to help others was characteristic of Jim, right up to his death in his 85th year.

An intelligent and thoughtful man, Jim was aware of how much more he might have achieved, had he been able to complete his formal education. He made up for this to the best of his ability by a lifelong process of self-study and continuing training.

During the depression years, Jim worked as a labourer in Glasgow's Parkhead Forge. He vividly remembered the long queues of unemployed men waiting outside the gates, hoping that an exhausted labourer would collapse or quit and give them, in turn, a chance to earn a few shillings before they too were discarded. This experience influenced him profoundly, and for the rest of his life he was a strong believer in the need for workers to organise to defend themselves against exploitation. At the same time, he strongly disapproved of unions abusing their strength to extort unreasonable or destructive concessions from their employers.

Jim was a fiercely moral man, whose values and approaches to child-rearing were more Victorian than Edwardian. He was the personification of the Protestant work ethic, and continued to work until well into his 80's. A thoroughgoing perfectionist – 'If a job's worth doing, it's worth doing well!' – Jim demanded perfection from his family, fostering in all of them a sense of inadequacy which, in one way, drove them to prove themselves, and in another, barred them from achieving their full potential. Christine was acutely conscious of her lack of self-confidence, and it is a constantly recurring theme in her journals.

Jim was scornful of the abilities of women. He used to say: 'There are two classes of people who should never see a job half done – the one's a fool, and the other's a woman!' Although he mellowed later, in his younger years Jim was easily frustrated and prone to violent outbursts of temper which he controlled only with great difficulty. At times, this made him a frightening figure to his young offspring.

The world outside the family home never saw these aspects of Jim's personality. He was always gracious and gentlemanly, sober, competent and industrious, considerate of his staff and respectful to superiors without undue deference. In turn, he was respected and liked by subordinates and bosses alike. He was always willing to give up his leisure time to undertake projects for friends or church, and to do more than his share of whatever work needed doing.

It seems likely that his efforts to live up to his own values created stress which could only be allowed to surface in the protected and private environment of the family home. It would be doing Jim a great injustice to suggest that he was callous or inconsiderate of his family's well-being. He set extremely high standards for himself, and felt constrained to pass on those values to his children. Men brought up in his time were expected to suppress their softer feelings. He had great difficulty showing the love that he certainly had for his family. (Alistair can remember seeing his father cry only once, at the funeral of Jim's youngest sister, also called Christine.) The strict upbringing he imposed on his children was his way of demonstrating his love for them, by setting them on the paths of morality and virtue. He also did everything in his power to provide the material necessities of a healthy life, a difficult task for a working class man in the years before the welfare state provided some security of income through periods of unemployment or illness.

When Jim married Jessie Ritchie in 1937 he was determined that his children would have the chance to grow up in a safer and healthier environment than the inner city, which was all that most working class men could aspire to. He purchased a small, semi-detached house in a new development right on the edge of the country near Clarkston, Renfrewshire. The housing estate was built on land previously part of the Stamperland farm, and the Taylor house backed onto the White Cart river, which to the present day forms the demarcation line between town and country.

When Christine started attending Netherlee Primary School she soon became close friends with another Stamperland girl, Sheena Cook. Christine's friendship with Sheena contributed later to a fateful decision.

All three Taylor children enjoyed the freedom of playing 'down the back', as they called the steep wooded area between the house and the river. The river at this point made a great loop, flowing on three sides of an open field area, now overgrown with hawthorn trees. In the 1940s it produced nothing but an annual crop of blackberries, and a thick cover of dry grass in late summer, usually set on fire by juvenile arsonists for sport. Behind the field, another wooded escarpment led upwards to a higher plateau, stretching towards the village of Carmunnock, which, during the war years, boasted an anti-aircraft battery and a camp occupied by Italian prisoners of war. The POWs, who worked on the local farms, seemed both harmless and friendly to the curious children of the neighbourhood.

The guns, of course, were an irresistible attraction to the local boys, at least in daylight. At night, during air raids, the guns would roar into action. At the terrifying first clamour of the sirens, Jim and Jessie, or frequently Jessie alone, if Jim was on night shift, would rouse their two sleeping children and descend to the cellar, which Jim had outfitted as a crude bomb shelter. Lowering the trapdoor which led down from the kitchen, they would wait fearfully, listening to the gunfire, and praying for the 'all clear' siren.

Wartime or not, the woods were off-limits to most of the neighbourhood children, their parents fearing that they might drown in the river. In winter, when it was in spate, it all too often claimed young victims. Jim and Jessie made a conscious decision that they would not mollycoddle their children, preferring to give them a great deal of freedom so that they would develop self-reliance and independence.

Unlike many brothers and sisters, Alistair and Christine were close friends who enjoyed doing things together. They climbed trees, lit fires, built 'dens' and generally revelled in the adventure playground that lay open to them on the banks of the Cart and in the surrounding fields and woods. Christine's love of adventure and the countryside must have received its initial impetus here.

Holidays contributed too. The family never had much spare money in the early years, so most holidays were strictly 'budget' affairs. A very popular destination was a farm near the Ayrshire village of Ballantrae, where Joe Callendar, the farmer, allowed holidaymakers to pitch their tents in a cow pasture, or to rent a small hut which was once a hen house. Christine and Alistair loved the farm. They could hunt for eggs under the gorse bushes, marvel at the skills of the sheepdogs, watch the shearing and dipping of the sheep and help in the haymaking. A favourite pastime was beachcombing, exploring the tidal pools of a little bay cut into the rugged promontory of Downan Head, said to have been the haunt of smugglers in the bad old days. Sheena Cook's parents also had a little cottage in Lendalfoot, not far from Ballantrae, so contact between the Taylor and Cook families continued during the school holidays.

Recognising that education was the only reliable route out of the working class, Jim pushed all three children to strive for the best possible marks in school and to continue their education after secondary school. Alistair went to university, and obtained degrees in Physics and Engineering. Christine and Elspeth both trained as primary school teachers. All three became compulsive readers, a habit which was encouraged when Christine married Alan Witcutt, who drove a travelling library van round the rural areas of Lanarkshire. Alan brought home many books which had been removed from circulation, and as a result, the whole family built very eclectic home libraries of their own.

Jim and Jessie also passed on to their offspring a love of music and an inherited ability to play musical instruments. Jim was a trained singer with a good tenor voice. Jessie, a competent pianist, was his accompanist. When Jim's friend Donald Ross and his wife Mary came to visit, it was time for a traditional musical evening. Few of today's families, raised on the canned entertainment of television and video tapes, can even imagine such an evening. These occasions were marvellous fun. Everyone performed, as soloist and in duets. Jim and Donald sang humorous duets about dilettante French policemen who preferred catching butterflies to criminals. Jessie and Alistair played piano duets.

All the children took piano lessons from Margaret McCulloch, a childhood friend of Jessie's. Margaret was a gentle woman and a capable

The Taylor family, around 1954

teacher, but it was Jim who insisted that the children carry out their daily practice without fail, a task which sometimes called for a heavy hand or a loud voice. Alistair, Christine and Elspeth all did well in many music festival competitions, and progressed through the examinations of the Associated Board of the Royal Schools of Music, with generally above-average results. More importantly, they all acquired an abiding love of music, whether listening or performing.

Although for many years Jim used a bicycle to get to work, this did not discourage him from cycling for pleasure, an enjoyment he passed on to Christine and Alistair. He introduced them to the Scottish Youth Hostels Association when they were barely in their teens, and Christine continued to tour Scotland by bicycle until the year of her death. One of her dreams was to become the warden of a remote youth hostel in the Highlands, an idea she might have pursued in her retirement years, had she lived. She adored the Highlands, and could imagine nothing better than to spend her life there hiking, climbing or cycling.

Religion played a major role in the lives of the Taylor family. Jim and Jessie were members of a little-known fundamentalist sect called the Christadelphians, and brought their children up in the precepts of their faith. Christadelphians believe that the Bible is the wholly inspired Word of God, and look to it to guide their daily lives. Their interpretation is strict and exclusive. Although the passage of years has softened many of the more austere aspects of Christadelphian values, in the 1940s and 1950s it was difficult for young Christadelphians to avoid a visible isolation from their less constrained contemporaries. The church disapproved of frivolous entertainment, such as dancing or going to the cinema. Christadelphians were required to marry other Christadelphians. Church attendance on Sundays was taken for granted.

Christine was the product of this environment. She inherited her father's strong sense of duty, his love of music, education and the outdoors. She grew up intelligent, artistic, thoughtful and compassionate, but was plagued throughout her life by self-doubts and feelings of inadequacy. In the following chapters, we will draw on her journals and letters to tell, mostly in her own words, the story of her life from her earliest memories through school years and work, marriage to Alan Witcutt and motherhood, to retirement and her fateful decision to become involved in relief operations in the war-torn wreckage of Yugoslavia.

2

Books, Boyfriends and Bibles

Christine started writing her first journal on 21st September, 1958:

'In seven days time, I will be 17½ years of age. Of the first seven years of my life, I remember very little; only the rigours of rationing and the lack of many of the luxuries which make life so much easier these days. I'm told that when I was only a few months old, the air raids were at their worst. Dad, like so many other fathers, had to do fire watching, while Mum handled her young family as best as she could. Strange to say, the war has left no scars on my memory, as it did to so many young 'war children'. Perhaps this is because we lived, and still do, in a quiet suburban area where there was nothing to bomb or destroy, for however vile the Germans were reputed to be, I still cannot believe that they would wilfully destroy the lives of defenceless women and children.

At the age of twelve, I graduated to the top class in the first year of Eastwood School. I was still quite clever, although I had not then discovered my ability at English and thought Mathematics would be *my* subject. I was quiet and shy of everybody, especially boys. This was my peak year in everything. I came fourth in my year at school, won the Lanarkshire Music Festival, and played in the Festival Concert. I narrowly missed winning my class in the Glasgow Festival, being beaten by only one mark. I spent my holidays in Scripture Union camp at Brora, and came home fired with religious fervour – the first interest I had taken in religion in any form.

In October of that year, I competed unsuccessfully in the Electricity Board Cooking Competition, but showed myself in better light by winning an essay competition run in conjunction with it. The prize was a bicycle and

Christine's prize in the Electricity Board Essay Competition

I was suitably thrilled, especially when the rector, with an eye for good publicity for the school as usual, announced my win from the platform at Assembly. Winning the bicycle, however, was my last taste of fame, for after it I settled down into peaceful mediocrity, unlike Alistair, who still continued to amaze everyone with success after success in music as well as at school. I must admit I was a bit jealous but I think it was charged with admiration too.

I intended to leave school at Easter in third year, but Dad wouldn't let me, wanting, I suppose, to give me the chances that he didn't get. I'm glad now that I did stay on, as I feel I would have been miserable working in an office or a shop, having had a little experience now of working during my holidays. My third year at school was fun. By this time, I had received a little recognition as far as writing was concerned, and I won the English prize together with Ann Sloss.'

This was the year that Christine participated in her first Christadelphian youth gathering and preaching campaign, in the east coast town of Montrose. She was very moved by the experience, and resolved to be baptized, the ritual that marked full membership of the church. 'When I got home, however, Dad wasn't so sure and attempted to dissuade me – successfully. I know now that I was carried away by the heat of the moment.'

However, she continued her involvement in youth group activities, including evangelical campaigns in various towns and cities, social gatherings and conventions, and working in hospitals and old folks' homes. A key concern for every young Christadelphian was to find a mate, from a rather limited pool of candidates. The Christadelphian Church has a fairly small membership, scattered across the length and breadth of the British Isles (and in other countries overseas), with its greatest concentration in the Birmingham area. The youth gatherings were essential to bring young people together, and many stable and happy marriages resulted from such opportunities to meet. Christine, however, did not limit herself to dating only Christadelphians at this period of her life.

'In the last three days of my holiday at Maidens, I got to know Leslie, who worked around the caravan site. He was an extremely romantic fifteen year old, who took me for moonlight walks along the shore, and made extravagant declarations which little Christine lapped up in approved fashion. From him I received my first proposal of marriage. We parted sorrowfully, but after four weeks of romantic love letters, I had had quite enough and broke off relations quite firmly and definitely.

One of the big events of my young life occurred when, at the age of fourteen, I was asked out by the idol of the third year girls, for whom I had had a "thing" for several months. His charming words to me when he showed me the scout dance ticket were: "Hey, nig nog – how about it?" Naturally I was overcome by his delicate invitation and accepted forthwith. Life was idyllic for about three months. . . .'

This relationship went the way of all Christine's other teenage romances, each one leaving her a little sadder but not much wiser. Fortunately, she had other pastimes which provided more long term satisfaction. Already at fourteen, she and her friend Sheena began youth hostelling together, travelling by bicycle to hostels in the south west of Scotland, as far away as Stranraer and Gatehouse of Fleet. That year also saw her first visit to the Highlands, a three-week cycling holiday with Alistair, now seventeen, which took them to Inverness, Ullapool, Gairloch, Inveralligan and Glenelg. This holiday was memorable, not just for the magnificent scenery, but for the incredible heatwave weather, the very unusual drought, and the unbelievable ferocity of the 'clegs' (horse flies) along some of the mountain passes which the two traversed. This was the last time that Christine and Alistair cycled together until June 1993, only five weeks before her death.

The following summer, Christine and Sheena headed north on their bicycles for a hostelling holiday that took them as far as Fochabers. There they befriended four young English motor cyclists. Their paths crossed several times during the remainder of the trip, at the end of which Christine and Phil Corbett, a London policeman, agreed to write to each other.

That year, Christine was forced to admit defeat in her study of Mathematics. Demoted to the Lower Mathematics programme, she also dropped Science.

'Instead, I took Lower Art, and acquitted myself quite well in it, much to the surprise of Miss Ewart, my art teacher, who kept on saying how glad she was I had dropped Science. I would have said that she was no more glad than was Miss Dungavel who had taken me for Physics. I'll always remember her words when I told her; with a relieved smile she said "I think you're very wise." '

At Easter time in 1958, Christine and Phil went motorcyling in the Highlands.

'On my birthday, Sheena and I went to the Alhambra to see the ballet, out of the goodness of Mum's heart, as she provided the tickets. The performances were all quite delightful, and completely rekindled my taste for ballet and music.

Four days later, Phil arrived, much to the delight of the family and neighbours as they had something to gossip about at last. We made for Alltsaigh in blinding sleet and bitter cold. I had a chilly night's sleep *sans* hot water bottle and was well and truly wakened by my icy cold, straight down from the snow-caps splash next morning.

We set out early for Ullapool, where we hoped to find bed and breakfast. Unfortunately, we couldn't get two singles anywhere – one landlady did offer us a double and was rather shocked when she found out that we were not married – but finally the warden, bless 'er 'eart, at the hostel allowed us to stay there in company with two stranded German girls and a Scottish Youth Hostels Association official and his family.'

Later, the weather improved, and they ended up at Gairloch, Wester Ross.

'We went past Loch Maree and Slioch. The water of the loch was an incredible blue, a blue such as I have never seen before but hope I will witness many times in years to come. The sun was gloriously warm, more like summer than early spring, and I was just itching to get in swimming. At last we reached the beach, and stripping off our heavy sweaters we got into swim suits. I think I was out and in the water a dozen times that day, although Phil only managed three. I just don't seem to feel the cold and I hate sand on my wet body, so I kept on going out and in.

We arranged to rise at 6.00 am, but silly thought she'd try some worm-catching and, mistaking the hour, got up at 5.00 am.

What heavenly solitude at that hour, with everything shrouded in a pall of soft grey, shadows showing mauve and lilac on the cool still water. Soundless solitude in which I was almost afraid to breathe for fear of breaking the silent spell of the foreboding mountains all around. A bird cried high up on the Ben and, once more having power in my limbs, I returned to the hostel to wake Phil. But I bear the memory yet. That country has my soul. Only there do I feel the powerful import of love for my country. It is so solemn I can scarcely breathe.'

Perhaps her prose was a little 'purple', but her later life attested to the accuracy of the sentiment. Back to school again, she worked on the school magazine for the rest of the term.

'End of term went literally with a bang – crackling powder down the aisles at the prizegiving, stink bombs in the class rooms, abductions from the girls' common room, all the bells in the school stopped. Last but not least, a triumphal procession with instruments ranging from bagpipes to tin lids, round the school – at least as far as we got – then it was all over and my schooldays behind me!'

Christine's friend, Sheena, went to Germany and found a job in Heidelberg. Christine decided to go to Jordanhill College to train as a teacher. She obtained a summer job in a store, but found it extremely boring. The highlight of that summer was another visit by Phil and his friend Dave, who took Christine and Sheena on motorcycle rides to Balmaha and other beauty spots near Glasgow. Christine enjoyed riding at 87 mph on the pillion of Dave's motorcycle, her highest speed yet. When her job finished at the end of August, she headed south to spend two weeks with Phil, first in London and later touring in the West Country. This was her first visit to the capital city, which she found rather overwhelming.

'There is a definite, commanding power behind this great city where one could walk about dressed in skins without anyone noticing anything strange about it. During the first week, we pottered around, seeing all the recognised places to see, and visiting so many museums that I thought my feet would fall off. We saw, in point of fact, too much of interest and beauty for it all to be taken in.'

The holiday over, it was time to return to Glasgow and teacher training. Jordanhill College proved to be less forbidding than Christine had feared, but still failed to treat its students as responsible adults.

'We soon found that it wasn't very far removed from school, and we rather resented, as we still do, the rigid discipline imposed upon us . . . . The main point in favour of college life seems to be that time passes quickly . . . . There is very little interest shared between lecturers and students and at first this indifference disturbed me. Soon however I learned its value – if they were indifferent to you, they didn't notice if you weren't there – a valuable thing indeed. Of my actual teaching the less that is said, the better. I gradually had to admit to myself that I just wasn't going to be brilliant and that anything I might achieve would only be achieved by dint of real hard work.'

Perhaps this disillusionment contributed to a new interest in literature. 'About this time, I conceived a passion for Dostoievsky and read several of his books. They are strange gloomy stories – some of them drawn from his own life – and they seem always to leave one with a bitter taste in one's mouth.'

Teacher training had one notable benefit for Christine. 'I was doing fairly well in Speech Training, and by way of a test had to give a talk lasting three minutes. It went down well, and I was satisfied. Strangely enough, I have very little fear of speaking before adults in that capacity – I even enjoy it. There is a tremendous thrill to be gained from holding an audience, feeling such control over them that they laugh when you want them to and are serious at the right time.' Never one to give herself unqualified praise, she added: 'In Speech Training, of course, an additional asset is that our audience is in sympathy with one, and probably all too ready to laugh to relieve the utter boredom of the class.'

Once her teaching practice started, things got worse.

'I felt that I had done not too badly but I wasn't a very good judge! Mr. Manson said that my subject matter was unsuitable, my discipline was lax and my attitude in general was too friendly; also my introduction was obtuse and confused. Of course I felt rather dumped. It is a failing of mine always to expect to be marvellous at once and I was again disappointed as I was obviously *not* a brilliant teacher and possibly not going to to be. I was annoyed at the play Manson put on my lack of confidence – I don't now, nor ever did feel shy in front of the kids – it was only the presence of Mr Manson which made me uncomfortable. Criticism is never pleasant and I frankly don't like it- constructive or not!'

Bad 'crits' continued, and Christine began to wonder if she should give up the thought of teaching. Relations with her father were also difficult.

'Dad went on holiday on Tuesday – he spent his holiday in customary fashion – working around the house and getting under people's skins – but that is a little unkind. Let's say that we got under his – if that's any better. After my grammar exam on Monday, I had decided to go to the swimming baths, but Dad had other ideas and a large and violent fight ensued after which I packed my case – but of course we eventually made things up, although the atmosphere was strained for days after.'

Once again, Christadelphian activities provided a distraction for a few days, but Christine, in a mood of self-doubt, found herself questioning her motives for wanting to join the church.

'I wish that I could get myself straightened out; I have so many high ideals, perhaps set myself too high a standard (if that can be done) then get so depressed at my inability to live up to it that I can't see the force of trying at all. . . . Do I wish to attain to the Kingdom of Heaven? Do I intend to serve my Creator for the sole purpose of being part of that Kingdom? Could my wish for a place in the Kingdom be merely part of a human's natural desire not to be ended for ever? Or do I associate myself with the body to please my relatives and to have a reasonable standing in their eyes? But all these questions will be answered some time, I suppose. At present my religion is something in the nature of a cloak which screens me from the things to which I have little inclination and allows me yet the companionship of a likeable crowd of high principled people.'

Christine eventually overcame her doubts sufficiently to apply for admission to the Christadelphian fellowship, and was baptized. But she continued to wrestle with these and similar questions, though she never relinquished her ties to the church. One thing that she never questioned was the set of Christian values she had been given by her Christadelphian upbringing, and they continued to guide her for the rest of her life.

Again back at college for the final term of the year, Mr Manson's harsh criticisms continued. He sent the head of the Methods Department out to hear Christine teach.

'The effect this had was to throw me into despair and paroxysms of grief – I was sure that I would be found wanting and be flung out dishonourably. I wanted to leave college – I hated it – I didn't know what I would do until June and I was sure to fail my exams anyway, etc., etc. In other words, I was pushed down and I just sat there moaning instead of getting up and doing something about it. Fortunately for me, friends and correspondents rallied round and knocked the nonsense out of me and, despite all my fears, my next two "crits" went quite well and as far as I can see I must be at least satisfactory if not brilliant.'

This passage is the first time in her journal that the expression 'get up and *do* something' appears. It became a guiding characteristic of Christine's life, and her perception that 'somebody ought to *do* something' about the miseries of the Bosnians was a direct cause of her involvement in relief operations. Like her father, that somebody was generally herself.

Around this time, both Alistair and Christine got a painful, if valuable, lesson in the importance of being able to judge character. The Taylors' next door neighbour, Miss Thompson, took in as boarders a pair of young men, Sam and Stan, who worked for a publishing company selling cookery books and encyclopedias door to door. Jim Taylor and one of Alistair's friends, John Nicholson, both expressed grave doubts as to the integrity of these gentlemen. Choosing to ignore this good advice, Alistair went to work with them, and was foolish enough to lend Sam all the money he received for his twenty first birthday. That was the last he saw of it. After Sam and Stan disappeared, leaving unpaid bills and debts everywhere, Christine wrote:

'They seemed a nice enough pair and we accepted them happily into our midst – enjoying the freshness they brought to the place. Unfortunately, they turned out to be a pair of heels of *la première classe* and although we're poorer, we're glad to see the back of them. Appearances, it seems, can be very deceptive, and quite often one's confidence in human nature's innate goodness can be sadly shattered.'

During that summer (1959), Christine finally made her decision to join the Christadelphians. This seemed to stabilise her, and opened a new phase in her life. Back at Jordanhill College again, she found herself feeling much better.

'My new-found confidence is a wonderful thing – it helps me in so many ways to assert myself; I am no longer afraid to speak up in public and air my own views; I'm not afraid of little things like making telephone calls, travelling distances alone or talking to people who are more important than me. It seems as though a tremendous veil has been lifted from my life, allowing me to see clearly and when occasionally it settles on me again, I realise the joy of being without it. I suppose it's all part of slowly coming to maturity – physically and spiritually – but although I have gained from this maturity, I can't help a slight feeling of sorrow that I am leaving behind me part of my life which can never be recaptured – the time is swiftly coming when I shall have to be a responsible, self-reliant adult, the time when the foolishness of youth must be a thing of the past.

Occasionally there come to me nowadays moments of extraordinary clarity and vision. Exactly what I derive from them I do not know, but for a second or two only at a time I may feel the immensity of the world created by Him and my own smallness and lack of importance. It is a feeling of being withdrawn from myself, of complete detachment, when I see my surroundings with a depth of perception scarcely conceivable at other times. Perhaps it is a momentary closeness to God – the emotion felt high on a mountainside – alone with the wind and the sweet fresh air, the sensation of the earth beneath one's feet pulsating with a throbbing burning untouchable silence, where every breath seems a desecration of the moment.'

Her final year of studies kept Christine fully occupied, and it was not until August 1961 that she was able to return to her diary.

'I found my second year at college very hard work – not so much academically hard as onerous and wearying. The hard work, however, paid off and my history marks were high. My "crits" from Mr Irvine were fairly good, chiefly, I fancy, because I spent most of my time on infant work, at which I have always been best.

Reference to my college diary reminds me of an amusing incident when Sheena, Meta, Jan, Kate and I went to a dance at the Tech. We dined first at Meta's on chips and fried onions (which made us most alluring, I imagine!) then, in wellingtons and raincoats, as it was snowing, we made for the bus; we travelled into town half fare! I danced not once that night and came home thoroughly convinced of my own unattractiveness – as did Kate who suffered the same fate. I was so determined to be a worldly little miss and no one would give me the chance to be bad!!'

The Birmingham Christadelphians operate a nursing home for old people, many of whom are totally dependent on the nursing staff, making the work emotionally and physically very demanding. The permanent staff is supplemented by volunteers, mostly young Christadelphian women from all around the country. Christine spent part of the summer holidays working there, before returning to Jordanhill.

'Service at the Nursing Home made me certain of one thing – that I was grateful to God for my youth and my strength which enabled me to work there and that these gifts could be removed from me all too soon. I resolved to make good use of them while I had them.

I had a week at home before college began in October. As usual I had lots of fears and misgivings – especially about the long periods of teaching practice ahead – latterly these turned out to be most unfearful except for the usual "crits". It was grand fun meeting all the girls again – particularly our own special crowd – and we had plenty of time to get to know each other as we had more periods free than occupied.

Christine on her last day at Jordanhill College

Although attracted to the idea of Art, I decided to settle for my old favourite, English. Doctor Gatherer, a short, stocky, humorous little lecturer took the six of us for this. The first thing he did was cancel our Monday classes because he declared that Monday morning was no time for appreciating poetry! He then cancelled the first of the Thursday classes because he had to have his dinner then! He usually chatted to us for about 45 minutes of the next period – not necessarily about English (he once spent three quarters of an hour with us, discussing whether men should help with the washing up!) and then dismissed the class for the day. I would like to write a character sketch of Dr Gatherer, but I think it would be impossible, so many facets had he to his character. One could never be sure whether he was serious or in fun – at times his humour could be terribly dry and satirical – at other times just plain funny. He had a curious way of looking at you over his glasses in such a way as to make you drop your eyes with embarrassment. Most of us were afraid to speak in his class. For all that he really was a rather ugly little man, I think that he is one of the most attractive men I have ever met and I'm quite sure that all of us were really just a little bit in love with him.

During third year, I read five or six books a week – fiction and non-fiction, social and semi-political works, plays by modern authors like Miller and O'Neill and screeds of modern poetry. Dr Gatherer opened my eyes to the delights of Robert Graves and T S Eliot – the pleasures of drowning in glorious words, which through (sometimes) their very difficulty and obscurity are all the more enthralling and enchanting. Left to myself, I would read all the time – unfortunately there are other important things in life.

Other classes were much the same as previous years – Psychology was interesting in places, Education was abysmally boring, English (the formal lectures) was rather unexciting. Miss Bowie very nearly convinced me that Shakespeare was dreadful. Fortunately my own investigations nullified her shocking lectures. By June I knew that I had passed all my exams and was judged fit to be let loose on the world as a school teacher. I was rather disappointed at not getting any merits on my certificate – the system of awards is rather hard on the good all-rounders like Meta and I; it seems to cater more for those who are very good at one subject.

When Diploma Day came I was just as sad as anyone else at having to say my fond goodbyes, clear up my locker, and go.'

Student days were over, and soon it was 'back to school' again, this time in her new role as teacher. Before moving on to this phase of her life, we will mention two milestone events in 1961. One was Christine's first experience of losing a loved one.

'The New Year was heralded in by an unhappy series of events. In the same week, Johnny lost a young cousin in a road accident, Alistair had a friend terribly smashed up in a car crash and Aunt Chris, who for years was our favourite relation, had a fall on her way from work, took a haemorrhage and died. It was a terrible shock to all of us – really bringing home the reality and horror of death. How casually we treat other people's bereavements!'

Later that spring Christine, still only nineteen, was to meet a young Christadelphian man, whose interest in her was not altogether reciprocated at the time.

'In the few weeks prior to my graduation, things had been looking up in the boyfriend line. I went out twice with Alan Witcutt from Motherwell and he began to talk about getting serious. This rather frightened me as Alan is nearing 30, but I put him off as nicely as I could and later I wrote and told him definitely.'

3

Paradise
on
Earth

1961 to 1966 were momentous years in Christine's life. On 28th August 1961, she started work in her new job – teaching in Kirktonholme School in East Kilbride.

'I was given a Primary 4 class of fifty children and since then most of my waking hours have been involved in trying to keep them busy and quiet. At first I loathed teaching – the work was deadly tiring and unrewarding and I spent most evenings doing preparation for the next day's battle, but I like it a little better now and don't have to do quite so much out of school-hours work. I've been lucky in my school, and in the staff who are all very nice and helpful. Mr McCall is a gem who always serves me out a big dose of encouragement just when I need it most. If he is sincere, he seems to think I'm managing well and am really beginning to train my class – I jolly well hope so.'

On Christmas Day Christine received a letter from London. Her friend Phil had been married a few weeks earlier. Christine had greatly enjoyed her many trips with Phil over the years, and was going to miss the very comfortable friendship that they had shared. Phil remained a friend of the family, and never failed to visit Jim and Jessie when he was in Scotland.

The New Year brought a major upheaval to the Taylor family – a move to Edinburgh.

'We've lived in this house – as a family – twenty five years and now because Dad has received promotion, we are to leave it and go to

Edinburgh. My first feelings were elation and pleasure – a feeling of getting out of the rut and beginning anew; also joy because Dad had been successful and had received a big morale boost. But now I'm not so sure; what a lot one has to give up – a sentimental attachment to the house and the view from the back window – a love for the very walls and the memory of the experiences they have over-looked and shared. There's even the feeling that when Sheena comes back from Heidelberg, I won't be there to have long chats with her – or walks with the dog! Then there's the changing of schools when I'm so happy (and fortunate) at Kirktonholme – but that can be coped with more easily by me than by Elspeth, for whom the root-tearing process will be much worse.

But I'm sure all the same that the move will be a good thing – for one thing, we'll *have* to clear out full twenty five years accumulation of junk and rubbish from cupboard, drawer and garage! What a job – it will take months and we'll have to be quite ruthless!!

The urgent matter is to find a suitable house in Edinburgh: big enough but not too big, with a nice view and a garden, near a reasonable school for Elspeth (and, of course, for me) – what a hope!'

A few weeks later, Christine wrote:

'Furnished rooms in Edinburgh!! That's the latest and most hideous idea – while someone else lives in this house using our furniture which, battered and worn though it is, makes home out of where I live; while someone else makes grubby marks on the wall paper and oily fingerprints on the door and enjoys for seven years our secluded garden – *we* live in someone else's house – at home nowhere, belonging nowhere. What a hateful thought.'

'A period of almost two months separates today from these hysterical utterances above. As a matter of fact there is now very little or no danger of such a thing happening – for one thing furnished rooms are too expensive by far and for another Dad is really quite enjoying living in Edinburgh and we are rather looking forward to staying there.'

In her student years Christine had had many admirers, particularly among the young (mostly English) Christadelphians she met at youth gatherings and campaigns. But somehow these relationships never seemed to last, and after she started work the contacts with England diminished. It appears probable that she discouraged serious relationships with non-Christadelphians, and there were very few unattached Christadelphians in central Scotland. The problem of her continuing single state was never far from Christine's thoughts.

'The horizon is still clear of unsuspecting males for me to get my talons into – I'm beginning to think that it's hardly worth the trouble of bothering. I'm going to be a spinster and see the world and enjoy my life and be a success and . . . a lot of other stuff as well. After seeing what it costs in labour and money to buy a house I don't think I want to be saddled with that yet. Marriage is hardly 1% moonlight and roses, it seems. Besides I haven't been asked!!!!'

The disruptions of moving resulted in another gap in the diaries. In August 1964, Christine again began to write.

'More than two years have passed since I last wrote a diary. If anything, these have been most eventful years during which I have travelled to Yugoslavia, encountered many problems of different kinds and, I hope, grown and matured as a result of them. My thoughts and feelings about many fundamental things have changed, in some ways for the the best, in others, I'm afraid, for the worse.

My final term at Kirktonholme was happy and I left the school where I had made so many of my first mistakes with some sorrow, although I wasn't above gloating about the fact that I would soon have a class of thirty instead of fifty! I've always been lucky in my schools – being happy at work makes living much easier. I think it must be dreadful to set out each morning for six hours of drudgery and boredom. I even enjoy going to school now – a big change from my early attempts at the job. Anyway the painful experience of teaching fifty kids has been very valuable to me.'

That summer, Jessie, Christine and Elspeth joined Jim Taylor in Edinburgh, moving into a small house in Portobello, adjacent to Duddingston Park Golf Course. Elspeth went to school at Leith Academy, while Christine found a teaching post in the village of Ormiston, southeast of Edinburgh.

'At the end of August, I began school at Ormiston full of trepidation. I was rather shattered to learn that I was expected to teach Primary 5; I had thought it would be Primary 4 again, but really it wasn't very difficult, because I was just carrying on the work I'd done up until then. Soon, however, I settled into things and found that I didn't have to rush away to my classroom to mark books, because my marking speed had become so fast the previous year. I felt a bit odd hanging around the staff room on my own and used to go and read a book in my room. Kids are kids wherever you go, reacting the same way and nearly always predictable. My class had several very good workers and a tail of about half a dozen careless, untidy and pretty well hopeless ones. One of the funniest little lads couldn't remember the ends of sentences he started and frequently only wrote on half of his jotter page.'

In September Christine travelled to Coventry for her cousin's wedding. A woman of strong opinions, she was not impressed by Coventry Cathedral, considering it 'in all its outlandish splendour – a monument to modern art rather than a place of worship. I like the stained glass and the Epstein sculpture very much but think that the Graham Sutherland tapestry is hideous and the Cathedral spire ludicrous.'

In the early winter of 1962, the world was transfixed by the high drama of the Cuban Missile Crisis.

'Half the world thought we were due for the Third World War. I can well remember sitting listening to the 1 o'clock news in Mr Mann's study and feeling very scared indeed. I very nearly joined CND at that time as I felt they were at least *trying* to do something concrete about the whole messy business. But of course, the crisis subsided and the world forgot its fears and we in the staff room went back to wondering whether the road would be blocked by snow again by 4 o'clock.'

In 1964, Christine decided to visit her friend Sheena in Germany.

'Sheena wrote to me and suggested that, instead of my just visiting her in Heidelberg, we should go together to Yugoslavia, to the island on which she had spent so many happy days the previous year, at the home of Damir Perinić on the island of Hvar.'

In Heidelberg, Christine met Sheena's boyfriend Halim, an Albanian Muslim from Kosovo in southern Yugoslavia, who was studying medicine at Heidelberg University.

'We arranged to meet Halim and Issa, his brother, when they finished work. We had an ice and then walked down the Neckar where it was decided to take out two skiffs – one for Sheena and Halim, and the other for Issa and me – he spoke no English and very little French – I knew no German at all – it was very, very difficult but eventually he managed to get across that he would like to make a date with me for the next day, leaving me with the problem of explaining in German that we were leaving for Munich the next day. . . I think I got it across at last, but it *was* difficult!!

When we returned to Heidelberg later, I found myself a lot in Issa's company – I like him for his gentleness (a contrast to his brother) and quiet studiousness. Unfortunately he imagined himself in love with me and my German was just not adequate for the explanations and arguments this provoked. I'm afraid I must have hurt Issa – but I was never cut out to be a Muslim wife!'

After hitch-hiking from Heidelberg to the Austrian university town of

Graz, the two young women travelled by train to Zagreb (the capital of Croatia) and on to Split. A two-hour ferry crossing took them to the Dalmatian island of Hvar.

'As we stepped off the boat, we were grabbed and hugged by blonde, red-bearded Damir. Things moved quickly then; in no time we were in a pleasant room in a clean, fresh house high up on the hill. Our landlady – Buzolic Simeta – was charming and couldn't do enough for us. We decided to swim first, then eat and later sleep off the long journey, so that we were fresh to walk over to Mala Vira the next day. The bliss of sleeping on a 7ft square double bed, between dazzlingly white sheets in a comfortable room can't really be appreciated till one has slept the previous night on the floor of a train corridor! We woke early (or rather, I did) the next morning with the scent of fresh-cut lavender floating in the open window – people start work there at 5:30 am and "fjaca"[siesta] in the afternoon when the heat is broiling.

We began our walk over to Mala Vira around 8.00 am and even then it was so hot that we paused every three minutes for breath. But it was worth the struggle across the rough, stony, overgrown track when, scratched and sweating, we arrived to a greeting of tremendous warmth and friendliness. A glass of schnapps, which made me rather tiddly, and a heavenly swim, which made me even more tiddly, and we were ready for a rest in the sun followed by a delicious meal of fresh caught fish. It is impossible to describe life at Mala Vira – it has to be experienced in all its delightful warmth and lethargy. . . there is no hurry because the day is long and peaceful, and the night is cool and calm and there is always a tomorrow to do what has not been done today. The Yugoslavians really know how to relax and enjoy simple pleasures.

We slept over in Hvar village and each day, as early as Sheena would rise, we walked the 3 – 4 kms across the hill to Mala Vira. We fished, sailed in Damir's boat, "Florian", swam, sunbathed, played cards and talked. The Perinić's holiday home is a 13th century cottage with three rooms. It was originally inhabited by monks. There are two houses nearby but the house is virtually isolated. Although the area is more or less deserted, it is not without historical interest – Ionian burial mounds and many Roman remains – Damir has fished up many fragments of pottery, which with his artist's eye for beauty in simple things he has decorated with a splash of colour here – a few black lines there, and made them into beautiful ornaments. Also on the whitewashed wall of the simple interior of the cottage are the "skeletons" of three lobsters, bleached golden in the sun – they look fantastic.

We slept there two nights – I went out to get the nets in in the pale grey 4.30 am light of the dawn – glorious – one takes one's toothbrush too and brushes one's teeth in the cold salt water. Sometimes we walked out to the end of the peninsula, to Mal Kontenat where stark white rocks slope smooth and shiny into the sea. And there, as everywhere else round these wonderful coasts, one could just swim along with one's face under water and see thousands of multi-coloured fish and sea-creatures – starfish and black spiky sea urchins – beautiful but lethal – even the loathsome sea cucumbers which cover the nets with disgusting sticky fluid.

Mala Vira has no modern conveniences – the drinking water is stored in a cistern under the stone floor of the house – the toilet facilities are the trees – dishes are washed in the sea. Food tastes wonderful, the sea is so warm you could stay in it for hours – sleep is deep and satisfying and getting up in the morning is no problem.

The hospitality of the Yugoslavs – whether Serb or Croat, Communist or Catholic, is amazing by our standards. Our landlady treated us like honoured guests – she and her husband kept us talking one night and kept on refilling our glasses with sticky, golden Prochek until I tottered rather than walked home to bed. That was the night I was caught in the toilet in my "baby dolls" while the whole family waited outside to get in. I felt rather embarrassed as I scuttled past.

Christine and Sheena sampling a fine Yugoslavian wine with Damir's family on Hvar, 1964

One day we went on a two hours sail to Starigrad where Damir's aunt and uncle live in a windmill house. We left at 6.00 am and called for breakfast at the home of two old fishermen in the bay with the unpronounceable name of Lucisce. These were childhood friends of Barba Luka and greeted us very warmly, pressing us to a delicious meal of raw salted fish on bread soaked in olive oil and washed down with Bivanda – red local wine mixed with water. I politely and surreptitiously buried my fish in the sand!! This was a really poor house – they only had one cup and they slept among the nets in a filthy old attic – yet attached to the house was a small chapel – a shadow of more prosperous days.

There is one thing yet unmentioned – the dish Damir declares has the most superlative flavour of all, unbeatable for richness and deliciousness: none other than hobotnica – octopus – horrible to look at when uncooked – if anything, worse when floating orange-pink and glutinous in a sauce of red wine. I tasted about a square inch of a tentacle, but my stomach would have rebelled at any more. The sight of the suckers on the tentacles was quite enough. Our staple diet at Mala Vira was fish – boiled, baked and fried in various guises. Even I enjoyed it though I was never very enthusiastic about sucking the brains out or eating the fins and tail!!

The sail to Starigrad was perfect. To sit at the bow of a small boat dangling one's feet in the warm blue sea, caressed by the salt spray which dashes up and knowing that the sun will dry one instantly. To sing at the top of one's voice and not care who hears, as the little boat bounces over the waves – that is as near perfection as I can think. And later when the light has gone, to sit in a deck chair and look up at the millions of stars sparkling in the clear midnight-blue sky – that is peace – a God-present peace exalting one's mind above the trivial business of the day.'

Thoroughly captivated by the whole experience, Christine wrote a postcard to Elspeth.

'On the front of this PC, you see a picture of Paradise on Earth, because that's what this place is, a holiday island two hours by boat from Split. Here, we swim (in warm water), sunbathe, talk or sail in Damir's boat "Florian". This is the perfect way to live, and is made even better by the wonderful food that Damir's mother cooks for us. The weather is unbelievably hot, and from being "white as a cheese", as Damir's father described me on Wednesday, I am now red as a lobster, and kinda sore in places. Perhaps you could come here with me next summer – if you could save enough – and learn Croatian!!'

From Hvar, the girls went on to Venice, where they enjoyed a romantic interlude with two very chivalrous Italian boys.

'They were exceptionally good company and looked after us royally – carried our bags, bought us Cokes – necessary as the temperature was about 100 degrees F – and paid our fares back to our hotel. It's hard to make one feel beautiful when one's hair is a wreck, one's nose peeling and one's feet dirty because one's been walking barefoot, but our charming escorts managed it, while also making us conspicuous by imitating a dog on the bus – Beppi made the noises and Pietro went around saying "Good dog, here dog, good boy"; soon everyone was looking for the non-existent dog. They were not the least bit interested in our hotel and refused to come to the door with us – most surprising for Italian men who are usually very persistent.

They invited us to spend the evening with them but we had a previous arrangement with Milica [a professor of Italian at Belgrade University] to go out in a gondola. Great – they had their *own* gondola and she could come too!! They escorted us to the station to find her and we duly introduced them, feeling rather self-conscious at how quickly we'd got ourselves "picked-up". We found that our professor had meanwhile found some friends and was going to spend the evening with them so whether we liked it or not our gondola trip was to be a foursome. Milica, by the way, thoroughly approved of our friends and thought they were true gentlemen.

We had a meal and a wash and a much needed relaxation and were ready to meet our escorts at 9.00 pm. They hadn't only brought the gondola, but also provided the romantic music – guitar and accordion and the refreshments: juicy red sugar melon, ice cream, red wine and Coca Cola served through a window at 2 o'clock in the morning; ice cold beer straight from the bottle as the boat glided through the dark canals. Could anything be more romantic than having someone sing Santa Lucia or Volare to you as you rock in your gondola below the Bridge of Sighs? I loved every minute of it – nothing could have been added to improve our enchanted evening.

At one point we "parked" in a side canal to eat our melon as Pietro serenaded us on his accordion; at another, we were nearly frightened out of our wits when a cat jumped out of a second storey window into the canal, swam across and scrabbled up the other side and disappeared; when we were tied up under the Bridge of Sighs quite a crowd gathered to listen to the boys singing – we felt quite important!! By 2.00 am as we were making our way back to our hotel most of the tourists and the straw-hatted, striped-shirted gondoliers had disappeared and all was quiet and still except for the soft splashing of the waves against the gondola as Pietro poled us along – very hard work, incidentally. We were escorted right to the door, they shook hands with us, thanked us for a memorable evening and departed – no exchange of addresses or anything – and that way it was kept perfect, though in some ways it would have been pleasant to keep in touch as they had been so kind to us – the nicest boys we met.'

Later that year, Sheena returned to Glasgow to marry her boyfriend,

Halim. She became a Muslim, and eventually the couple and their baby daughter, Lirije, moved back to Kosovo.

'Sheena's wedding day like the rest of the days that week was wet – very wet and windy. Kate did my hair for it and then gave me a run up – this was just as well as I'd have had precious little left of my hairdo if she hadn't. Things were in a turmoil in Sheena's house – everyone flapping around trying to get ready – all wanting into the bathroom at once. The wedding took place in the Registrar's Office at Eastwood Toll and it must have been one of the oddest the Registrar had ever performed. As Halim didn't understand English, Sheena had to translate everything into German and Halim, himself, wanted to say his bit in Albanian as well. The best man ran around taking photographs and re-arranging the furniture and flowers to suit. Shortly afterwards, Sheena and Halim went back to Heidelberg.'

Christine began to feel more and more dissatisfied about her own life as, one by one, all her friends began to get married. Around this time, at a Christadelphian social event in Glasgow, she ran into an old boyfriend.

'I was late and very flustered when I arrived and had just plunked down to drink a much needed cup of tea when an old friend, Alan Witcutt, came up and we chatted for a while before someone else started talking to him and we drifted away. Once I had admired Alan a lot and couldn't understand why he'd never married – I knew he'd had a girlfriend a few years previously but had no idea what had happened in between. I wasn't at my best on that occasion, conscious again I suppose of all the happy couples around and feeling very much my single state.'

A few weeks later, she attended Sunday morning service at Alan's church.

'I must admit, we didn't arrive at Motherwell completely by accident. I wanted to see Alan again and to make up my mind whether I would like to start again the friendship we had had a few years previously when I'd got the feeling he was quite interested in me. I had always felt so much at ease in his company that I wondered if maybe, both of us being alone, we could perhaps team up.'

Christine's church was to hold its annual November barbecue soon after this meeting.

'This gave me my excuse and I wrote to Alan and invited him through. This way he could understand the invitation the way he wanted to; if he wanted to think of it as an invitation to something more, he could, and if not, then all I had done was invite him to a barbecue. I spent several hours composing letters to him then tearing them up, until I felt it was good enough and then after I posted it, I wished that I hadn't. However he accepted, and when I saw him at Glasgow a week before the barbecue we had quite a long chat, and Johnny and Pat [close friends of Christine's] invited him back to supper. When Johnny took him to his train, he made it clear that he liked me at lot but he didn't want to run into anything without thinking about it first. By bedtime, J. and P. had the wedding day arranged!!!'

After the barbecue Christine was disappointed when Alan refused to come back to supper. She thought that this was his nice way of saying 'nothing doing'. However, two years later, her diary recorded:

'The central theme of this period of my life will, of course, be Alan. After my fears at the outset were allayed, our relationship grew swiftly in depth and I think both of us by the Christmas of 1964 felt committed to each other, knowing this was not a fleeting friendship but something which was going to last. In some ways it was, I think, a step towards maturity for both

Christine's first solo run on her scooter. Near Ormiston, March 1965

of us. There was no fiery passion, none of the "love-symptoms" which books lead one to expect (and which invariably turn out to be short lived), but simply a strong affection, a common interest, a security which I for one very much needed. Our difference in ages, though considerable, did not seem to matter at all.'

As their relationship developed, Christine regularly travelled to Wishaw to visit Alan, and soon bought a motor scooter.

'The next few months were spent learning to drive. As usual, I was a very slow starter and Alan must have had a few very uncomfortable moments on the pillion. However, by late March I was safe enough to drive to school on it and shortly afterwards began to use it to go to Wishaw at weekends. This was a great improvement on the 27 bus. I think if our romance had foundered on anything, it would have been those freezing cold bus journeys lasting nearly 2 hours which I undertook every second weekend that winter. Even on my first trip it only took me 1   hours. Alan used his motor bike all winter, sometimes even on icy roads and it sometimes seemed perversely that it always rained on Friday evenings!!'

On 4th September 1965, Christine and Alan got engaged 'to everyone's delight and no one's surprise.' The first problem was to decide where to live after they were married. After considering various alternatives, they decided to fix up the upper flat of Alan's parents' home in Wishaw, while Mr and Mrs Witcutt (senior) continued to live downstairs. At the end of the 1965-66 school year, it was time for Christine to say goodbye to Ormiston.

'I was very sad to leave Ormiston where I had been so happy for four years. I regretted leaving behind the friends I had made but I knew also that I was leaving a fairly easy job with small classes perhaps to get in return fifty per class in a Lanarkshire school. (It didn't turn out quite as badly as I thought it might, but I certainly have to work a good deal harder.) We had the usual end of term rush with concerts, puppet shows and prize giving, but all too soon I was travelling home for the last time on the Ormiston bus – a little uncertain of what lay ahead, as always before when I've changed the direction of my life, but confident that everything would work out right.'

Christine and Alan were married on 10th September 1966.

'On our wedding day it rained – heavily! Alan was nearly unable to come having almost been crushed by the car against the garage wall. Elspeth and I fell out minutes before the taxi arrived because I didn't like the way she'd fixed my hair. Eventually when I did arrive at the church, I was so early that the photographer wasn't there and the photographs had to be posed afterwards! The hall was packed – so packed that I got out of step with Dad rounding the corner to go up the centre aisle and never quite got into step again!

George [the Christadelphian preacher conducting the marriage service] forgot to give the bridal party hymn sheets, so while the rest of the congregation had one each *we* had to share. Then Elspeth's nose began to run. I could hear her sniffing surreptitiously and had to work out a way to pass her my handkerchief without everyone noticing. The funny thing was that most folk thought that she was having a wee cry to herself!'

Soon it was time to leave for their honeymoon, which turned out to be a catalogue of disasters. After a leisurely trip south in the white Vauxhall Viva car they had bought a few months earlier, they arrived in Dover at midnight, and found accommodation for the night in the Central Hotel.

'For once something went well. We were only a short distance from the channel ferry terminal and, with very little fuss and a much shorter crossing than we had anticipated, we were in France. Alan had never driven on the continent before, and Boulogne was a rather fearsome introduction; but before long we were heading southwards by one of the main routes. We stopped briefly in a village to buy fruit, bread and a bottle of detergent, which taxed my rusty school French to the full and caused quite a bit of merriment!

We noticed that traffic seems to move on average faster in France than at home, but that they seem to drive more sensibly. Alan quickly learned to increase his normal driving speed by about 20 mph and to waste no time getting back into lane after overtaking. There were two things which presented difficulty, "priorité à droite" in towns and the incredibly boring sameness of the road – mile after mile of dead straight, level, tree-lined road with featureless fields on either side occasionally broken by a battered, unpainted, depressing, little village. Further south a little more variety was evident, but always there is this air of gentle disintegration.

At this point we still did not appreciate the distance we had to cover and spent long hours picnicking and on one occasion chatting (in execrable French) to an old peasant woman who adored the British and insisted on giving us some of the oranges and grapes which she had laboriously cycled probably 10 miles to buy at the local market.

We stayed our first night in France at a place called Chauny – in the Station Hotel. The accommodation was simple in the extreme, but the meal we had later was first class. We discovered that night why 'Station' Hotel – trains running past our window all night. This was the first of many disturbed nights we had. The French seem to believe in building their hotels on main roads – and in running heavy transport along them at 70 mph all night long!!

I suppose what I like least of all about travel abroad is the lack of knowledge about local ways of doing things. We never knew when to tip and when not to tip; we never knew whether our meal would be two, three or four courses as we weren't always given a menu. My difficulty in understanding and making myself understood didn't help this. Less ridiculously sensitive people than I would probably sail happily on, careless of what impression they were making, but I've always tried not to behave in such a way as to make people despise the British bourgeoisie any more than they already do!

By this time we were beginning to have carburettor trouble and Alan was constantly cleaning and blowing at it. Every few miles it seemed we had to stop and take the tools out again and, to make matters worse, he wasn't feeling very well. Our second night we spent in a hotel near Dijon – a hotel with hard bolsters and noisy plumbing!! The next morning we were embarrassed to discover that we had not enough French currency to pay our bill and had to rush into Dijon to the Credit Lyonnais and cash a cheque!

We were still having car trouble and in the middle of a traffic jam in Aix-en-Provence, the car stopped altogether and would not restart. This was a problem. First we pushed the car on to the pavement. There was a car park next to us but the entrance was uphill. So I stayed with the car while Alan went off to find a garage with a note explaining our difficulty. Fortunately someone spoke English and he soon cleared the blocked jet.

We stayed that night at Orange – a small market town with some very well preserved Roman remains. This was the first night we had camped. It was a pleasant little site and very quiet but with the usual French plumbing. To flush the toilet one had to depress one lever while pulling another and the result of these endeavours was not really very satisfactory!!

The next day we parked the car in Orange and went sightseeing and shopping. Our purchases made, we endeavoured to return to the car – only to find we were quite lost. Alan was sure we had come one way – I was convinced of the opposite. Eventually after about an hour we retraced our steps to a garage at which we had bought petrol on our way in and from thence we found the car – the temperature inside was 120 degrees Fahrenheit!!

Still the car was giving trouble. Near Avignon, the indicators (so necessary when one is driving a right hand drive car) packed in. A fuse had blown and this happened every time we flicked the indicators. A garage mechanic finally fixed this and with the warm blue seas of the Cote d'Azur clear in our minds' eye we pressed on southwards. We had a meal in a small town – lasagne verde and rosé wine, and by 5 o'clock had sighted the Mediterranean. We had our first swim at La Ciotat then determined to find a good camp site near the coast.

We chose Les Oliviers – an unfortunate choice as we combined comparative isolation with a nearby railway line and masses of mosquitoes. Already we were realizing that our dirty little "bivvy" tent was a little out of place with all the splendid frame tents around and we preferred to get as far away from them as possible.

That night I heard footsteps outside the tent and shot into a terrified wakefulness – but they went away. This made me nervous of camping sites and we decided to look for a pension the next night which we spent near Hyeres. For the first time that night, Alan was really ill and I had to finish my meal alone. When I joined him in our room it was only to listen for hours to the staff gossiping in the kitchen door – and some of the time they were discussing us!!

We spent the day in the mountains near Cogolin where it was cooler. We picnicked and I washed my hair in a mountain stream. This area on the Corniche des Maures is often ravaged by forest fires and the evidence of this was to be seen in the charred trees around us.

In the afternoon we stopped near a vineyard to take photographs and bought for pence a huge basinful of grapes (5 francs actually). We never finished them, there were so many, and if we'd had any sense we should have realised that Alan certainly shouldn't have been eating them.

We carried on to Grimaud – a hilltop fortress town which we explored, briefly visited St Tropez but didn't stay as it was raining, then set off round the coast through Ramatuelle – another hilltop town and after a glorious sunset found a small hotel – Pension Beau Sejour and booked in there. The room and the meals were simple but adequate, but the real delight of the place was that our room had a balcony with a view out to the Isles of Levant and there we would sit to have our breakfast every morning.

After a rather chilly day on the beautiful but exposed beach at Cavalaire we discovered a tiny beach at a place called Gigaro. This, we decided, was the France we had come so far to find – a narrow bay, coarse sand shelving swiftly into warm seas, a snorkel swimmer's paradise. By now I was not so afraid to wear my bikini but was having terrible trouble with my hair which was long and would not stay tidy – hardly surprising considering that I had worn rollers every night for years and had now, of course stopped!

After a few days at Gigaro we decided to take a trip down the coast so that at least we could say we had seen Cannes, Nice and Juan les Pins. We were not impressed!!

As Alan was still feeling seedy we were now taking the utmost precautions with our food but this it seemed was not enough. After a night at St Pons where I was very badly bitten by mosquitoes and another in a camp site at Miramar on the gorgeous Cote D'Esterel (where a hedgehog had a go at our Carnation Milk which we left outside the tent in preparation for the morning) we came west again to Gigaro. We both had haircuts on the way. We had no lunch as it was too hot to be hungry, and have never been able to explain why Alan suddenly took ill with violent food poisoning on the beach at Gigaro.

I asked some people nearby for help and they arranged for a taxi to take him to hospital in St Tropez. The rest of the day was a nightmare. I had no idea what was wrong with him but he seemed terribly ill. We had to leave the car behind – I took only money and passports, not even a jersey to wear – although a Madame Isaacs who was living in a villa nearby arranged for the Garage du Littoral to pick it up and garage it for us till we were able to collect it again. The car ride to St Tropez was agony. They took him first to a Clinique where the nurses were all nuns but they said they could do nothing and behaved as though it was all rather amusing. He was then loaded into a van which was more like a baker's van than an ambulance and off we went again. I tried to find out from the driver where he was taking us but either he couldn't understand me or wouldn't make the effort. We arrived at another building and he indicated I should get out – when I did he closed the door and drove off. I really broke then and howled. Someone pointed to a flight of steps and when I got down there I found the ambulance waiting. They seemed to think at first that he had broken something as they took him into an X-ray room but eventually light dawned and he was taken into a small room with two beds.

From then on it was injections, bed pans, sick bowls, and I was expected to help. We did not see a doctor – no one told us what was wrong with him – no one suggested I might like a cup of coffee – he was given no water though he had a deadly thirst and I was afraid to give him tap water in case it was impure – to cap everything evening was drawing in and I was cold and I didn't know where I was going to spend the night – I certainly didn't want to book into a hotel with no luggage and on my own. However, they gave me a deck chair to sleep on but with the cold and the two hourly interruptions for more injections, to say nothing of my empty stomach and my worry, I slept little.

By the morning Alan was better but very weak. We felt however that he was well enough to leave and we were worried about the cost of treatment, for although we were insured, our ready cash was very limited. Once again we met with evasion – we had to see the doctor first and he came at 5 o'clock. By 7.00 pm he still hadn't come and Madame Isaacs who had been kind enough to come and fetch us by car had to leave. When he *did* arrive he simply kept on saying "not tonight – tomorrow!" and went out having hardly even glanced in Alan's direction let alone examined him.

The next day was Sunday 25th. I packed and waited until a nurse came in. "Sorry – you can't leave – it is Sunday – the office is closed!" We visualised another boring day – we imagined another £5 added to the bill – we thought of Madame Isaacs making another wasted journey, so we treated her with reciprocal nonchalance – "The doctor said we could go. We will return tomorrow and pay the bill." She shrugged and departed as did we a short time later in a dark green Fiat driven by Madame Isaacs' daughter. They took us to the garage and left, refusing all thanks as though they had done nothing when they had practically saved our lives!! The garage owner too was kind. He would take nothing for having looked after the car for us and was very helpful in such ways as he could be with our troubles with the car.

So finally we left the south of France with our indicators not working and a wine cork stuck in the carburettor, where Alan's endeavours had stripped a screw. We had most of our troubles fixed at Avignon and were five miles from Boulogne on our way home when disaster struck again when a lorry tipped rubble on to us on a sharp bend, bursting our headlamp and mashing up the front of the car. Sick, we boarded the boat for Dover a day early and rested easier of mind and digestion that night in a Bed and Breakfast there.

We were not sorry to be going home; despite the wet weather – despite the busy roads – we had had our fill. What of our honeymoon then? I hope I *never* have a disastrous holiday like that again. I did like some things about France – notably the delicious bread and the good wine which costs very little – but to go again. . . I doubt it!'

4

Midnight Musings

Marriage transformed Christine's life. There was no time now to maintain her diary, resulting in a gap of over twenty years in the journal record.

Christine and Alan did in fact go back to France many times for family camping holidays. The passing years produced two children – Paul, born in 1970, and Julie, three years later. A growing family required more space, so they moved, first to a council flat in Gowkthrapple, and later to a semi-detached house in Muirhouse. Alan's father Jack died in 1980. In April 1984, Mabel Witcutt, Alan's mother, chose to move into sheltered housing, allowing Christine, Alan, Paul and Julie to return to the family home. Over the next few years they carried out extensive remodelling and refurnishing. Christine set about beautifying the garden, which became her pride and joy.

After the wedding and honeymoon Christine started teaching at Lammermuir Primary School in Wishaw, the first of several local schools which benefited from her devoted efforts to open the minds and expand the horizons of her young charges. She took six months off work for the births of each of her children, but otherwise she taught uninterruptedly until 1992, when she took up an offer of early retirement.

Like the Taylors', the Witcutts' holidays were usually simple and economical. The favourite choices were a rented caravan at Southend on the Kintyre Peninsula, and camping at Brighouse Bay in Kircudbrightshire. In October 1983, Christine, hoping to recreate the magic of her first visit twenty years earlier, persuaded Alan to holiday on the island of Korcula in Yugoslavia. This was the only time that they went abroad to stay in a resort hotel. Christine was terribly disappointed. The resort was nearly empty of guests. The weather was poor; the region was poor; the people were poor; the service was poor. Electricity was available 24 hours a day in the hotel,

Christine, Alan, Paul and Julie, hiking near Wanlockhead, Dumfries and Galloway, around 1982

while the local residents had daily power cuts. The shops had little to sell; the hotel food was adequate, but lacking in variety. Schools seem to provide only part-time education for the children. There was no overt hostility towards foreign visitors, but the locals were not particularly friendly. What Christine was seeing was the economic failure of Tito's Communist system. After that holiday, the Witcutts went back to camping holidays – usually in France.

On New Year's Eve in 1989, Christine again started writing a daily journal, but was unable to sustain it for long. After the first few days, she found herself adding to it only on the occasions when insomnia drove her from her bed in the middle of the night. Few people have a particularly positive outlook on life at such times, so it is not surprising that we find a rather sombre bias in her writing. It was, in fact, a very difficult period in Christine's life, during which she experienced severe symptoms of menopause and had to cope with the illness and death of several family members and close friends. While the outside world saw only her usual smiling countenance, her journal reflects her inner stress.

'A new attempt to keep some sort of journal – starting fairly appropriately at the end of the decade. This last year has been better personally than the one before. I will start by reviewing some of the significant milestones of 1989.

Alan retired unexpectedly early, but with the promise that his health will not deteriorate rapidly and that money will be adequate because of the enhancement of his pension and the invalidity allowance from the DHSS. Mum moving to Balerno caused a great deal of extra work. The fact that Mum is happy with her home and her neighbours is a just reward for all our hard work. Paul, after weeks of waiting, was accepted for nursing training and is enjoying the work so far. He has grown up considerably, seems to have a fairly responsible attitude to life, and is really no worry at all to us apart from still being a smoker. Julie passed O-grades in English A, History A, Biology A, Art B, Maths B, French 2 and will sit Highers in the first four. She is a delightful girl, very strong willed, but that's no disability these days. She is maturing nicely, but as yet, apart from hero-worshipping pop stars, stays free of attachment to boys.

The highlights of the year for me were the success of the school show "Mary Poppins", the amount of cycling I've managed to do, the improved state of house and garden and not least, the Ben Eighe climb in the summer. I've felt a bit more settled and contented personally and have tried to cultivate realistic expectations for my future, but I do sometimes wonder where, if anywhere, my life is headed. I'd like to keep up outdoor activities, but also get to a few more concerts and perhaps become more musically involved somewhere. I will not settle easily into old age but will fight it all the way.

1989 has seen massive world changes. Russia under Gorbachev has opened its doors to the West and this has encouraged the movements in Poland, Czechoslovakia, East Germany and Romania – only the latter being accompanied by much bloodshed. The Berlin Wall is down, but what will happen now is hard to foretell. There is much world wide suffering. China has clamped down on changes there in the aftermath of the Tiananmen Square massacre. Cambodia may yet have much to suffer if Pol Pot is allowed to go unchecked. Forcible repatriation of Vietnam refugees from Hong Kong seems awful, if inevitable. Starvation again stalks in war torn Ethiopia. Earthquakes in San Francisco killed many, but not as many as there might have been. The people, including Aunt Inez and family, still fear for the major quake which must come some time. America has invaded Panama – why? The rain forests in South America are still being burned to clear them. Greenpeace and Friends of the Earth have effected an incredible "Green" Revolution, but no one knows whether coming changes are too late to stop the inevitable. We at home have tried to help in a small way by using household products which don't harm the environment, and

Julie is now fully vegetarian.

On the home front, the Conservative Government continues to push through its largely unpopular policies. This is especially so in Scotland. Poll tax is an unfair tax which benefits the rich and penalises the poor. We have paid – to my shame, I haven't the guts not to – but many can't or won't pay and the law will have to take action to obtain the money. Electricity and water are being privatised, and the NHS has been threatened by various moves, not the least being doctors' contracts – payment by number of patients. School Boards in Scotland are now a fact; they are not representative, and may only be a money wasting exercise. Teacher assessment – laughable in view of the shortage of recruits – is scheduled and head teachers are now to be administrators and part-time accountants. Many many people are homeless and despairing. They sleep rough in every major city. Young folk cannot leave unsuitable jobs or they get no benefits. Minimum wages have been abolished. Students in 1991 will have to borrow money to supplement their grants, thus leaving them with huge debts at the beginning of their working lives.

Hopes for 1990: Good health for all of us and enough money to get by. Four A passes for Julie and success for Paul and Mark [Elspeth's son] too. Contentment for Alan and two cars that give no trouble. For me: more confidence, less whining and two inches off my hips! Many good days of climbing, walking, cycling. A beautiful garden in the summer and the love of our friends. For the world: Moves towards democracy, socialism and peace everywhere – world moves to protect the environment. Hope.

New Year's Day, 1990. Brilliant start to New Year – sometime during the night my car was broken into and vandalised – locks damaged and all wiring just cut through. Hogmanay otherwise was quiet. Both kids out with their friends, leaving Darby and Joan at home!! Spent today with Mum, Elspeth and Mark. Joint effort on food. Quite pleasant and relaxed.

3rd January 1990. Another gloomy day as was yesterday. My car is now mobile again, Alan having connected up the cut wires. I enter and leave by the passenger door – awkward in a tight skirt!

I find increasingly a feeling of alienation from whatever it is makes ordinary people tick. That sounds as though I feel myself superior – maybe I do, but in an inferior sort of way. I sit and listen politely to others being incredibly boring, and am afraid to speak at length myself in case I do the same. Why, when there are so many fascinating subjects, is normal conversation not more interesting? Probably it's because you need to have something in common with the person you are trying to communicate with, and you need the confidence to feel that you are making sense – or even the confidence to be wrong and occasionally make a fool of yourself without feeling small. I read so much and try hard to be informed, but seem not to be able to retain what I read or to bring it back in conversation – unlike Alistair who retains everything and has perfect recall. Can't help feeling sometimes that I missed out somewhere with heredity. Neither incredibly clever like Alistair nor glamourous like Elspeth. Not even sure I can spell any more! Funny how three children of the same family can be so similar and yet so different. Perhaps something to do with spouses, but probably it's predetermined by heredity or environment. There have been short periods in my life when I've felt really good about what I was doing and confident in my capabilities. Thinking back to when these times were, it is impossible not to jump to certain conclusions, some of these not very attractive.

Certainly there is no use moaning about irretrievable actions – life is about accepting and getting on with the job, while never giving in to a belief that life cannot be improved with effort. At the moment I'm some distance from any kind of crossroads. Perhaps in a few years there will be more options open, and by then I should be past the present hormonal upset and into calmer waters – pity that has to wait until relative middle age . . . though there's no way I mean to give in gracefully to that.

Curious how putting thoughts down on paper seems a pretentious thing to do. For whom, after all, am I writing? I suppose I hope that in expressing thoughts and ideas in some way I may sort them out and exorcise some of the hang-ups which have been fouling up my full enjoyment in living. I need to be able to believe I am a worthwhile person, an interesting companion, a valuable worker. At the moment, that at times is difficult to do. What this work does not want to be is a reiteration of the same things – going nowhere. It remains to be seen if it can develop into something worthwhile or be simply bin material.

Watched "Out of Africa" this evening. Robert Redford is so beautiful. Good subject for consideration – what is it that makes one man irresistible to most women when in almost everything else we have individual tastes?

4th January 1990. Following up what I wrote yesterday, I have decided to list the most attractive males I can think of – not in any order of merit but just as they occur to me: Alan Alda, Tom Conti, Robert Redford – all still very attractive even in middle age; Anthony Andrews (not sure about him); Paul Newman; Albert Finney (when young); Richard Burton (before he got involved with Liz Taylor). [Also included were a number of personal acquaintances, who will not be identified here.] For me, though, the biggest attraction beyond the instant charm of good looks, or even the niceness of a caring nature, is perhaps that of the good talker. I wonder how universal my list would be – at least the film stars and show biz people. Obviously the younger generation would list different people, and the older would choose the men who were young and in fashion when they were young.

Curious that, although at near fifty I don't feel older, I don't presume to admire many men younger than myself. A man would, I think, choose from younger women, regardless of fitness or availability. How hard I find it to come to terms with the ageing process, nevertheless. Such sadness to have to accept that heads no longer turn, and all that is left is the memory of past conquests. Clearly confidence must come from a different source now.

6th January 1990. Rereading the foregoing is slightly humiliating – it's all so trivial and badly written. The idea [of this diary] will probably die the death from want of talent, but also, as we are always being told in Education, for want of a suitable audience. Diarists of the past probably wrote for the audience who will read of their lives and hopes at some future date. I can't really envisage saying anything of sufficient import to divert my descendants. Also my inborn sense of privacy is probably going to stop me writing the truth. Truth can be hurtful, and I see it as a form of self indulgence to put down on paper things that might offend or upset – or even, and perhaps this is the crux of the matter, reveal *me* as far from perfect – even that last phrase is a euphemism for what I really mean.

Today has been a funny day. I've been quite unsettled, partly because school starts on Monday and the need to tie up all the holiday ends usually paralyses my ability to do anything at all. I eventually realized that my lack of energy was due to two things – working hard yesterday tidying up tree and decorations and then staying up late watching Meryl Streep and Robert DeNiro in a rather good film, and not having any coffee earlier today. A good big mug full, with a chunk of Christmas cake, got the adrenalin going again. So much for my intentions of cutting down on food (to lose the desired two inches from the thighs!)

I wish I could be more humorous in what I write. Pat would have made this account into an exaggerated catalogue of disasters. I have to be pedestrian and write it straight. At least I'm not boring anyone, as no one is going to read it.

8th Jan 1990. 1.20 am. Insomnia. One of those nights when the brain refuses to shut down. Relentlessly it regurgitates the same insoluble problems, relives the imagined slight, replans the possible – or totally unlikely – future. How is it that a normally comfortable bed can become an overheated, wrinkled platform tilted to just the right angle from the horizontal to make it quite impossible to lie in any position without discomfort? Who filled the pillows with tennis balls and coated the pillow cases with a tacky, sweaty substance which makes it as comfortable as burying the face in a plastic bag? Why does the telephone downstairs seem to keep ringing and what has happened to our normally taciturn clock to make it click in such an irritating way? Think of something restful. "I will arise and go now, And go to Innisfree." Lord, Alan's turned over and is starting to produce his incredible repertoire of sleeping sounds: whistles, puffs, snorts, grunts, gurgles. Perhaps I should get up and head for the front room settee. But the sleeping bag will be cold and maybe full of spiders from being kept under the stairs. I could fill a hot water bottle – but Julie used all the hot water for her bath. I'd have to boil a kettle. Oh good, he's turned on his side. I think maybe I'll drop off now. Not a chance. I'd go and make hot chocolate but there's none. Maybe a quick whisky – but I've got to go to work tomorrow. The snoring's starting again. I'll have to get up, go downstairs, read, write this diary. Try to sleep again in half an hour or so. Why is it that insomniacs always have husbands who snore? It's funny how as soon as you get up, all the rotating thoughts disappear. Problems which are insoluble in the horizontal seem to vanish in the vertical.

Called Ann C. yesterday. Ann isn't getting her early retirement – not likely really when there's such a shortage of teachers, though I've never known Edinburgh to be short before. I'll probably be stymied in a few years too. Missed the boat as usual. She seemed really disappointed. When you've set your mind to something, it's hard when it doesn't work out for you.

I'm reading a book just now called the "Gradual Vegetarian". I'm developing an increasing distaste for meat and can see myself changing over totally like Julie. The problem boils down to cooking two sets of food. Life is complex enough without that.

Walter A. phoned to ask why they hadn't had a card from Alan's mother. We obviously forgot to tell him – and yet in the back of my mind I seem to think we did. Lilian M. [his sister] has lost her eldest son from cancer. That makes the nth person in two years who's departed by that route. Makes you think.

13th January 1990. Turned out on Wednesday for Local Association Union Meeting. I'm not sure why I go. I accomplish nothing by being there and half the time am far from sure what they are talking about. Once again I've missed County Committee on Saturday. Perhaps a useless delegate is better than none, but I'm not sure.

Wednesday evening was Overtown's first School Board meeting and we had been *instructed* to attend to meet the Board members. My first mistake was agreeing, my second, washing my hair first! We sat from 7.30 pm till 9.40 pm in the staffroom waiting to be ushered in to meet this group – all of whom we've met before! What a fiasco. The fact that none of us officially complained shows what a pusillanimous lot we are are. *And* I missed "Mash"!

So another difficult week is over. I wish I could be more settled and contented. In some ways I am for a time and then this itch to change things, to change myself arrives again. Begone dull care – or self doubt and its accomplices. Don't I deserve a bit of tranquillity? How sorry for myself I am. Count the blessings! (Note how platitude follows platitude.) I have a kind, helpful husband who is really making an effort to do some of the things I nag him about and two super kids, a lovely house and more than adequate cash. I have a good job with fair earning capacity, etc., etc. What more really should I expect?

16th January 1990. Foul day today. Rain and high winds – three wet breaks at school. Not nice. Apart from that, feeling fine – total recovery. Thought today it might be pleasant to go to Vancouver [to visit Alistair] for summer hols. Initial thought was to take Mum but this could mean we'd be limited in what we could see. It seems a selfish thought but a realistic one. Alan would quite like to go to Florida to see his people there. I can see no reason why he shouldn't go, though I'm not keen to accompany him. Maybe this is the answer to our holiday problems. I could go hill-walking and he could fly to USA.

21st January 1990. 6.50 pm. So much for keeping a daily diary! It would, I suppose be foolish to think that something notable would happen every day. What effectively happens is that when interesting things are going on, time to write a diary is limited. All this seems to indicate that last week was a momentous week. Sadly this was not true. Nothing much happened except that the weather was exceptionally foul and I have been feeling rather tired and suffering from severe eyestrain. This finally has led me to do what I should have done a year ago and order new specs. The cost of £148 was not less than I expected, which was why I took so long. I hope they do the trick – and also manage to look nice. I spent plenty time choosing the frames.

Still discussing the question of holidays. Alan is really keen to go to USA, and seems not to mind going on his own. It would free me to spend my holiday doing what I want. Thinking about this over the weekend I have resolved(!!) that when the weather starts to improve, I'm going to get fit by climbing Tinto every weekend. It'll no doubt end like all other similar resolutions.

Workwise – I think my theories on the function of education are out of step. I know there are others like me that think that the main purpose is to make children feel that learning is pleasurable – that the world is a wonderful place – woolly minded liberalism probably – a get-out of having to organise properly maybe! In fact, I think it's not as much what is to be taught as who is doing the teaching. In a profession comprising 30,000+ teachers, how many of us have the power to delight and inspire? Most of us are mere hacks. But now and again I get the act together and do something I think is worthwhile, and no doubt others are the same.

Listening to the readings [in church] today, I was wondering whether the Psalms were King David's diary. He seems to have suffered from similar persecution complexes to me – and be just about as guilt ridden. I wonder if he felt that he was being pretentious writing all that stuff about his innermost thoughts and feelings. Lamentably my diary will never have the literary value of the Psalms.

15th March 1990. 12.45 am. A sleep eluding night so I might as well do something. Nearly two months has passed since this book was put away in its hidey-hole under the chest of drawers. So much for writing regularly!

The weather during January, February and March has been horrendously foul. The winds have howled incessantly. There has been widespread damage from flooding and a lot of structural damage and destruction of trees in the south of England. Fortunately we've emerged so far unscathed, though it is blowing a gale again tonight. The worst aspect has been the continual (and continuous) rain – weeks of wet intervals – weeks without a blink of sunshine or a snippet of blue sky. More than 120 inches of rain have fallen on Glasgow in the past three months – as much as usually falls in Fort William in a year. Yet spring and the flowers are struggling through, and two days ago our first daffodil opened in the garden.

Gorbachev has been made a virtual dictator of Russia – let's hope he's as good as we think he is. The Iraquis have hanged a British journalist. The government suffered a defeat over Health Service Legislation affecting old people (later sadly reversed) and the Poll Tax and Student Loans are causing many demonstrations and riots in England. It (the Poll Tax) must be the most unpopular law ever.

21st April 1990. 2.20 am. Having tried, unsuccessfully to get to sleep for an hour and a half, have come downstairs for a milky drink, in the hope that it, and tiring myself out writing this, might eventually get me back to sleep. I don't know why I'm not tired – I've been working really hard all week. Finding a list, penned last September, of all the things needed in the house, I was most distressed to discover that the only one accomplished was the replacement of the terminal balls on the staircase. Tonight I've been stripping the outside of the living room door prior to repairing the decorative mouldings chiselled away by Alan's father when he flush panelled some of the doors some years ago. (My family and other vandals!!) The previous night I repainted most of the hall door frames and skirtings and the night before I emulsioned the ceilings, a paler shade to try to lighten the hall. I'm not sure I like the light colour, but it will do just now.

Our vegetarianism is going pretty well, though sometimes it's a bit of a drag having to cook. We're becoming fairly adept at some of the easier recipes and have tried a few more complicated ones with reasonable success. However, we eat a lot of cheese and eggs and I'm not too sure how good these are – particularly for me at my age. How awful. I shall be 50 next birthday!!

Troubles continue in the world around us too. Lithuania and Russia are locked in a power struggle. Lithuania have declared independence from Russia, who have responded by cutting off their supplies of power. None of the Western nations are prepared to antagonise the Russians by being seen to help overtly. It's anyone's guess how it will end.

Saturday, 31st March saw terrible riots in London over the Poll Tax. I have no love for the police, but the violence was quite out of order and seemed to be preplanned by a very small number of demonstrators. Perhaps the police provoked it – they certainly have before. The demonstration in Glasgow, in contrast, was quiet, orderly and good natured. There must be a reason for this, I suppose. One wonders how long Thatcher's government can continue to cope with the level of difficulties they are facing. They've even had to climb down over the National Curriculum. Unfortunately it is too long till the next election to feel sure about anything. It should be interesting to see the local election results.

TV has been full for weeks, it seems, of the riots at Strangeways Jail in Manchester. The conditions in the prison seem to have been awful, three men crammed in cells built for one and locked up 23 hours a day. At school I have to listen to the "shoot them off the roof" brigade. I think they forget that not all criminals are murderers and rapists and child molesters, and that many have not even been convicted but are on remand. Some crimes are pretty ghastly and many criminals are hard to feel sympathy for but, to me, the punishment is that they are locked up and deprived of freedom and somehow it ought to be possible still to allow them human dignity and even a chance to atone in some practical way. But the hardliners don't even think they should be allowed to study or to do anything pleasant. Surely there should be an element of education as well as simple punishment. Even in the days when simple crimes carried the death penalty, there were still criminals. It is very possible that it is genetically caused anyway.

I think I may be ready to try to go to sleep. All for now until the next sleepless night. Hope for something pleasant to write before them.'

The 1990 diary ended at this point. It was not until her retirement in the autumn of 1992 that Christine again took up her pen.

'Nearly twenty years have passed since I regularly kept a journal of the type which I hope this is going to be. About three years ago, I made an abortive attempt to write a more conventional diary, documenting family and world events and going into some detail of personal feelings about these. I succeeded partially for about six months and, on re-reading what was written then, I find that it does appear to have "worked", but only on a limited level, as I am quite incapable of being totally honest on paper, knowing that, at some future time, my writings may be read and reveal, even posthumously, things which I might prefer to remain concealed for a variety of reasons. I am reminded of a poem by Norman McCaig entitled "Private":

> How my friends would turn away
> from the ugly sounds coming from my mouth.
> . . . . .
> How they would wish back the
> clean white bandages
> that hid these ugly wounds.

Like my journals of the past (1956 to 1970), the intended audience will be anyone who is close enough to be trusted and interested enough to look. I suppose the question first to be answered is possibly, "Why the gap?" The answer is simple – bringing up a family, working full time, renovating at least two houses, caring for a large garden, keeping in touch with family and friends, snatching stolen moments for personal pursuits like reading, cycling and piano playing; caring for, and finally watching die, several close members of family and some dear friends – all these things have filled the days to the point where little time was left available for a somewhat useless activity like this. But, since September 31st and my retirement from paid employment, many more things have become possible and this journal is one of these.'

Christine and Alan had celebrated their twenty-fifth wedding anniversary in October, 1991. Julie was now 18, and had just started a two-year course in Interior Design at the College of Building and Printing in Glasgow. Paul, 22, was going into his final year of nursing training.

In the summer of 1991, Christine had made a pilgrimage to the Highlands, travelling alone by bicycle.

'That trip was the culmination of a desire to see, at first hand, the main areas devastated by the Highland Clearances and a wish to use my bike as a total means of transport in the way we used to employ it years ago. . . . It was an immensely satisfying trip from which I returned feeling much more confident – and a good deal thinner! I had no trouble with my bike and handled the physical demands of cycling in fairly severe conditions with very little trouble. I also coped well, after the first day, with being alone and learned that if you show yourself to be friendly and approachable, people will respond in the same fashion. The highlight of the trip, though, must have been meeting and travelling with Guido, a German (Bavarian) classics student from Nordlingen who had been studying for a year at Nottingham University. He stopped to help me identify the cause of an annoying squeak. We cycled together to Lochinver. Subsequently we met again at Dundonnel and finished our holiday together. Guido visited us at home for a few days and came again this year in September.

The End! . . . Retirement from Teaching (at last).

Since the teacher's pay dispute in the mid-eighties I have been growing steadily more disillusioned, not really with the children – although deterioration in general behaviour patterns has to be admitted. Whether these were due, as most people in teaching say, to a decline in the discipline of the home and, perhaps, of the wider community, the influence of violence in films and television, or merely an automatic return on the less structured patterns of class organisation and teacher expectation, is debatable. The answer is probably an amalgam of all of these. And to them I would add that the rising generation, unlike their predecessors, can see very little that is hopeful for their future in the world in which they must live. The high rates of youth unemployment almost guarantee that nearly half of today's school population will never work. Those who do will have to accept living under the constant threat of being found expendable – the "natural wastage" which this government dismisses as the price which has to be paid to revitalise our moribund economy. Even children who have been granted from the genetic pool sufficient intelligence to carry them into further education have no guarantee that, at the end of all the work and near starvation of being a student on a student loan (when grants are eventually replaced!), they will be able to work in their chosen field – or any other, for that matter.

There is no point in begging for the unattainable. With no coal, steel, railway-engine building, shipbuilding or any manufacturing industry to speak of, there is not going to be a miraculous improvement in the prospects of employment. Service industries and tourism will be what is left, but they too suffer when people have no money to buy. And these people have to stand by and watch a few lucky ones rake in all the money and live at a standard most of us can barely imagine. Witness to this is the pay rise awarded to himself by the Divisional Education Officer. In a region of decrepit school buildings and spiralling material costs he can afford for himself a *rise* of £35,000.

Government plans now include, if schools can be persuaded, opting out, and if they can't, the marvellous "delegated management", which in England has meant that some schools have already gone bankrupt or are having to sack teachers to continue functioning. Much essential money must already be raised by jumble sales and functions organised by parents and employing the children during the school day so that normal work is suspended. Add to this the amount of waste – equipment purchased but never used, textbooks unopened because the system does not allow the purchase of a book for each child, the group system, the increase in paper work forced on teachers despite the fact that they have argued that it serves no useful function and takes time and energy from actual teaching. A few years ago, very little of this, even if it was theory, was enforced. This freed the individual teacher to follow what suited her best instead of attempting to be a clone of the teacher next door.

My ten years at Castlehill [Primary School] were followed by a move to Overtown. I stopped being happy at Castlehill when being Union Rep. during the teachers' dispute put me in the front line. I saw my job as putting the facts as clearly as I could, across to the rest of the EIS [Educational Institute of Scotland] staff and, clearly, at times I was too forceful or made mistakes in other ways, for the result was an upset and divided staff. My standpoint since then has been to follow the course of action I thought correct, but not to try to force agreement from others. In some ways this has worked, but it is irksome when most of the time one is not supported, but when some issue arises which sends everyone up in arms, one is expected to rush about sorting it out for the rest. (At Overtown, I again became Union Rep. in a time of dispute, and the whole nasty cycle might have begun again if I'd let it.)

The Overtown move was a bit traumatic, especially as Alan's mother and my dad both died during my first year there and I was also struggling with drastic symptoms from the menopause. The kids were no better and, in some ways, much worse than the kids from Castlehill. There was an arrogance about them. The physical limitations of the building – lack of storage and working space – made teaching really difficult and having to find my way round new schemes of work was also tricky. But I survived, and after a year felt fairly comfortable and confident. Staff changed from year to year but everyone was fine and there was a lot of fun in the staffroom – although I really missed having someone else on the staff who was actually on my wavelength.

1990 – 91 saw me struggling with the worst class I have ever had. Every day was a battle of wills and it was literally unwise to turn one's back on any of them. Academically they were generally below standard, and so much time had to be spent working with individuals that every night saw me with stacks of marking. Despite a good end to the year with the play I wrote about the Highland Clearances being performed for the parents quite brilliantly by my "rotten shower", I really felt I had to start looking for alternatives to teaching.

The school year 1991 – 92 was fairly uneventful. My class was small, well behaved and easy to handle. With the interest in the German language having been encouraged by getting to know Guido, I embarked on a topic about Germany, doing a lot of reading about the country and its history. The nearness of Re-unification made it quite a high profile topic and I enjoyed it, even if the children did not. In connection with this I went to "twilight" classes in German at John Ogilvie High. I worked on my own at home and listened to tapes in the car. With luck I hope to continue this learning with the help of a Goethe Institut course later this year.

Frankly, by 1992, although I had a nice class, I was increasingly bored by the whole business and think, in spite of my efforts to be interesting and interested, that it was beginning to show. Then, a few weeks from the end of the summer term, in the middle of a virulent dispute with the Scottish Regional Council who were attempting to lengthen our hours and shorten our holidays and do away with all our employment protection, a letter suddenly arrived from the EIS saying that a deal had been reached which included a package of voluntary redundancies – or rather retirements from around 300 primary teachers over 50 – this to replace compulsory ones among secondary staff. I first phoned Alan to check if he'd be happy if I quit and, having assurance on that (but does he still think the same?), I phoned staffing. They hadn't even heard about it at this stage but phoned me back later.

When the form came in – to apply without obligation on either side, I filled it in. I then began trying to work out how we could cope financially with the drop in salary. It was a tricky one but we reckoned we'd manage if we cleared our debts and also Julie was given a full grant. By the end of June it was clear I could have my retirement package if I wanted it. The money was good but not brilliant and Julie would get her full grant. I thought hard all summer, receiving conflicting advice from all sorts of people – some hardly qualified by experience to comment.

I wasn't worried about filling my time – I can do that easily with my range of interests, but a little unsure of my self image when Christine Witcutt – teacher became Christine Witcutt – housewife. The rest is history. I took the plunge and have not yet seen any reason to regret it. Money is a little tighter, but I can cope. Alan and I can almost get on without driving each other crazy. If I've one complaint it's that I tend to do too much house work and it was never my aim to retire into kitchen drudgery.'

Retirement in September was immediately followed by a trip to Cornwall to visit an old friend, Johnny Wilson. In mid-October, a long-planned trip to Torridon to climb Liathach and Ben Eighe with Paul turned out to be a disappointment, due to appalling weather. 'The trip wasn't a total waste of time. I enjoyed being in company with Paul – something I hadn't done much of before, most of my walking having been done with Julie.' When 1993 arrived, the weather had not improved.

'The winter has been a bit wretched because of the awful January we've had – gales, storms, and floods almost without let. Sometimes I think I'm taking root on this chair on which I sit to read and write letters and journals and do my German. But spring will come and the bike will come out of the shed and it's the open road for me as often as I feel like it.'

In fact, spring brought a very different kind of open road, and the bike stayed in its shed, except for a few brief interludes.

5

Yugoslavia in Flames

On 25th June 1991, Croatia and Slovenia declared their independence from Yugoslavia. Two days later, the Serb-dominated Yugoslav People's Army (JNA) attacked Slovenia. The cycle of destruction and atrocity was begun. Slovenia was lucky. The JNA, far from its home base in Serbia, was surprised by the determined resistance of the Slovenes, and suffered from the low morale of conscripts who were unprepared to kill their Slovene countrymen. Under pressure from other European states, the Yugoslav government in Belgrade accepted the secession of Slovenia. Fewer than 100 Slovenes had died during the ten day crisis. Their sacrifice had helped create the first independent Slovene state in over 1,300 years.

It was now clear that the Yugoslav government had neither the will nor the means to keep the country together. The 600,000 strong Serb minority living in Croatia had watched in dread as Croatia moved towards separation. During the Second World War, half a million Serbs in Croatia and Bosnia had died at the hands of Croatian fascists. Determined that this would never happen again, Serbian paramilitary forces launched attacks on Croatian police stations and other government installations as soon as independence was declared. The JNA, no longer a Yugoslav institution but rather the army of Serbia, soon joined the fighting, with no strategic goal other than to punish the Croats. Destruction was pursued for its own sake. Croatia was devastated. By February 1992, over 10,000 people had been killed and over a million displaced. Atrocities had been committed by both sides.

The European Community, fearful of a return to the explosive instability of the Balkans before the First World War, at first tried to keep Yugoslavia together. As the situation in Croatia worsened in late 1991 and public pressure to stop the fighting grew, the EC finally accepted that disintegration was inevitable, and invited the republics of Yugoslavia to apply for recognition. In January 1992, the member countries of the European Community recognised the independence of Croatia and Slovenia. United Nations peace keepers were sent in to supervise the three Serb enclaves in Croatia, and the fighting there finally died down.

Bosnia (or more properly Bosnia-Hercegovina) and Macedonia had also applied for recognition, but their requests were denied. The head of the Arbitration Commission recommended a referendum on the future of Bosnia, which was held in March 1992. Croatian and Muslim Bosnians voted overwhelmingly in favour of independence. The 31% of ethnic Serbs living in Bosnia-Hercegovina, who favoured union with Serbia, boycotted the referendum, claiming that the Croats and Muslims were 'ganging up' on them.

Instead of voting, Serb paramilitary forces launched a savage campaign of violence against the Muslims and Croats. By May 1992, the Serbs controlled nearly 70% of the territory of Bosnia-Hercegovina. At first, the Bosnian Croats joined the Muslims in fighting the Serbs. It soon became clear that the international community favoured a partition plan which would allow the combatants to keep any territory they had gained. Deciding to join the land grab, the Croats, aided by the HVO, the newly formed 'self-defence' forces of Croatia, turned on their former allies.

The world now associates the name of Bosnia with concentration camps, torture, organised mass rape, mutilation, merciless bombardment of defenceless cities and a new expression: ethnic cleansing. The atrocities being carried out daily in so many towns and villages of former Yugoslavia horrify us all, and force us to ask: what could lead human beings to descend to such barbarity, to hate each other with such ferocity? Most people have no real idea why Yugoslavs are raping, torturing and slaughtering each other so savagely, when they seem to have lived together peacefully for nearly fifty years. The explanation lies in Yugoslavia's long and complicated history.

The name Yugoslavia means the land of the South Slavs. When Christine went there in 1964, that name had been in use for less than forty years. In fact, the country had not existed before 1918, when the Kingdom of the Serbs, Croats and Slovenes was formed out of the wreckage of the Austro-Hungarian and Turkish empires. From its very creation, the country had an ungovernable mixture of peoples, all with different histories, religions and prejudices or hatreds towards some of their countrymen.

Marshall Tito, the Communist dictator of Yugoslavia from 1945 until his death in 1980, was well aware of the powder keg of nationalist feelings that had to be contained. 'I am the leader of one country which has two alphabets, three languages, four religions and five nationalities, living in six republics surrounded by seven neighbours, a country in which live eight national minorities!', he once said.

In this chapter, we can give only a very brief overview of Yugoslavia's tragic and violent history. A more detailed account is given in the Appendix, for those who would like to study this fascinating story in more depth.

The mixture of peoples in Yugoslavia is the direct legacy of the many empires which have fought over this strategically-located land. Throughout history, imperialism has resulted in the mingling of diverse peoples and the creation of national boundaries which take no account of the ethnic mix within them, sowing the seeds of future conflicts. We see the results today in the former Soviet Union, in Africa and India, even in Canada.

Our story starts in 330 AD, when the emperor Constantine moved the capital of the Roman Empire to the Greek city of Byzantium (later known as Constantinople). Sixty five years later, reeling under the attacks of barbarian tribes in both the east and the west, the empire was divided in two. The western empire remained Catholic, while the Eastern, or Byzantine, Empire founded the Orthodox faith. The dividing line between the empires, and the religions, ran through Bosnia.

The Slav tribes, who originated in western Ukraine and Belorussia, migrated into Yugoslavia during the sixth and seventh centuries. The Croats and Slovenes settled in the north and west and became Roman Catholics. Independent Croatian and Slovenian states existed briefly, but for most of their history, Croats and Slovenes were subjects of the Habsburg or Austro-Hungarian Empire.

The Serbs came under the control of the Byzantine Empire, and were converted to the Orthodox faith. Over the centuries, they grew stronger, and eventually were able to throw off the rule of the Byzantines. Tsar Stefan Dušan the Mighty, the greatest of the medieval Serbian kings, assembled an empire which included Serbia, Montenegro, Albania, Macedonia, much of Dalmatia, and parts of Greece. Dušan's ambition was to take over the imperial throne of the Byzantine Empire and throw the Turks back from Europe, but he died suddenly in 1355, just when success seemed within his grasp. His empire soon disintegrated after his death.

Around the same time as the Slavs appeared in Yugoslavia, Mohammed was spreading his new religion of Islam. Within 80 years of his death in 632, the Muslims had conquered vast territories stretching from Persia to Spain. Over the centuries, the Muslims absorbed more and more. The Byzantine Empire held out against the Muslims for 800 years, but eventually fell to the Ottoman Turks in 1453.

The Turks continued their expansion into Europe. Within ten years of the fall of Constantinople, Serbia and Bosnia were defeated and occupied. The Bosnian Muslims are the descendants of Serbs and Croats who accepted Islam after the Turkish invasion. The converts harshly oppressed their Catholic and Orthodox countrymen, who were reduced to serfdom under the Ottoman rule. The Serbs had a saying: 'A Serb turned Turk is worse than a Turk!' (The Muslims of Kosovo are Albanians, not Slavs, brought in by the Turks to occupy land abandoned by Serbian refugees in the seventeenth century.)

Hungary fell in 1526 and was occupied by the Turks for 150 years. In 1683 the Turks beseiged Vienna, which was able to hold out and counterattack deep into Serbia. Many Serbs left Serbia when the Austrians withdrew to avoid reprisals from the returning Turks. The Austrians encouraged these Serbian refugees to settle in the liberated parts of Croatia, to act as a military buffer between the Habsburg and Ottoman empires. (The Serbs were allowed to retain their Orthodox religion, which kept them from being absorbed into the Catholic Croat population.) This strategy resulted in the large Serbian minority which still exists in Croatia, and was instrumental in creating the current gun culture of the Serbian people. Children are trained in the use of guns from an early age and a man who cannot use a weapon, or dislikes them, is an object of total derision to the average Serb.

Eventually, the Turkish empire began to crumble. Serbia became fully independent in 1878. Bosnia and Hercegovina were first occupied, and later annexed, by Austria. Serbia, which viewed Bosnia-Hercegovina as part of 'Greater Serbia', was outraged, and relations between Serbia and Austria deteriorated rapidly.

In June 1914, Austria, seeking an excuse to crush Serbia, provoked a crisis by holding military manoeuvres in eastern Bosnia. The Archduke Franz Ferdinand, heir to the Habsburg throne, was assassinated by a 'young Bosnian Serb' extremist, triggering the First World War, in which eight million men were to die over the next four years.

The Kingdom of Serbs, Croats and Slovenes rose from the ashes of the Great War and the wreckage of the Austro-Hungarian and Ottoman empires. From the beginning, the Croats deeply resented the overbearing centralism of the Serbs. Politics was dominated by regionalism, and violence reached right into the parliament chambers, when the founder and leader of the Croatian Peasant Party and four other Croat deputies were shot by a Montenegrin Serb deputy in 1928. Unable to rule democratically, King Alexander suspended the constitution and established a dictatorship. He renamed the country Yugoslavia, and eliminated the old names of Croatia, Serbia, etc. The new regions were named after rivers. Alexander's solution to the nationality problem was therefore to pretend that the nations no longer existed.

In Croatia, an extremist party called the Ustaše now appeared. Strongly pro-fascist, the Ustaše modelled their style and methods on Hitler's SS. Convinced that Croatia could never achieve independence unless Yugoslavia was destroyed, their principal tactics were terrorism and murder. In 1934, the Ustaše, working with other revolutionaries from Macedonia and Bulgaria, assassinated King Alexander in Marseilles.

Immediately following the creation of the Kingdom, a strong Communist party had developed, but was banned in 1921. The party went underground, and continued to grow under the leadership of Josip Broz, half Croat, half Slovene, better known as Marshall Tito.

At this point, poised on the brink of the Second World War, it is instructive to take stock of the relationships between the different ethnic groups in Yugoslavia. The imperialism of the Romans, the Byzantines, the Ottomans, the Hungarians and the Austrians had mixed Orthodox Serbs, Catholic Croats and Muslims inextricably together throughout the Yugoslav lands. Albanians had claims to Kosovo, Hungarians to Vojvodina, Italians to Istria and Dalmatia, Bulgarians and Macedonians to Macedonia, both Serbs and Croats to Bosnia and Hercegovina. Different languages and alphabets emphasised the divisions between these diverse groups.

All these groups viewed their respective religions as symbols of their national identity. The ancient schism between the Roman and the Eastern churches, aggravated by memories of the Fourth Crusade when western knights sacked and looted the Christian city of Constantinople, had left undying hostility between Croat and Serb. Long subjugation to the Turks and the Albanian presence in Kosovo fuelled the Serbs' hatred of the Muslims. Interestingly, the Croats did not seem to harbour any great antagonism towards the Muslims, probably because they had never been under the yoke of the Turks, but they hated the presence of so many Serbs in Croatia.

Despite the tensions between the many nationalities intermingled in Yugoslavia, there had never been any large scale violence between them. The legacy of hostility and distrust left by history is certainly understandable, but antagonism had not yet escalated to atrocity. The coming of the Nazis was to change that for ever.

Yugoslavia managed to stay out of the Second World War until April 1941. Prince Paul, the regent, was finally forced by Hitler's pressure to join the Axis Pact as a non-belligerent member. This outraged the Serbs, who carried out a military *coup d'état* and placed young King Peter on the throne. Hitler was furious, and ordered a merciless attack on Yugoslavia. Under the onslaught of 27 German divisions, the unprepared and ill-equipped royal army collapsed in ten days. Seventeen thousand Serbs were killed in the initial three day bombing of Belgrade.

Yugoslavia was now dismembered, Germany, Italy, Hungary, Albania and Bulgaria all annexing substantial areas of the country. Croatia became independent under the control of the fascist Ustaše, signed the Axis pact and declared war on the Allies and the Soviet Union. Serbia was governed by a puppet regime, controlled by the Nazis.

Resistance was soon organised by the fiercely royalist (Serbian) Četniks and by the Communist Partisans led by Tito. The Nazis responded by executing 100 hostages for every German killed by resistance fighters. In Kragujevac, the old capital of Serbia in the days of Prince Milos Obrenović, German soldiers shot 7,000 citizens, including 300 children and their teachers. The example set by these massacres of innocent civilians seems to have triggered in all factions of the Yugoslav population a regression to medieval savagery incomprehensible to civilised people.

Serbs were massacred in thousands everywhere, but their treatment at the hands of the (Croatian) Ustaše is almost beyond comprehension. The Ustaše plan to deal with the Serb minority in Croatia was simple – convert a third of them to Catholicism; drive another third out; and kill the rest. They undertook the last task with ghastly zeal – knifing, bludgeoning and hacking to death tens of thousands in concentration camps, and burning whole village populations alive in their Orthodox churches. Enough Muslims assisted the Ustaše to justify the creation of a special SS division for them. The number of Serbs killed by the Ustaše is generally believed to be around half a million.

The popular image of Tito and his Partisans, created mainly by Hollywood and British liaison officers parachuted into Yugoslavia, is of incredibly courageous and upright patriots, fighting against impossible odds to preserve the integrity of their country and to liberate it from the bloody oppression of the Nazis. In fact, while the Partisans were surely brave, and many of them may well have been Yugoslav patriots, Tito was fighting primarily for the cause of Communism, to impose that atheistic philosophy by force on the Catholic, Orthodox and Muslim citizens of Yugoslavia.

The chaos generated by the Nazi invasion played into Tito's hands. With the state and its infrastructure shattered, his disciplined force of Partisans would enable him to seize power in the vacuum left by the retreating Germans. For this strategy to work, he could not allow any other organised force to survive that might oppose his takeover. The truth of this assertion is supported by the fact that Tito was much more concerned with fighting the royalist Četniks than he was with attacking the Nazi occupiers. He actually went so far as to propose to Hitler that, if the Nazis would agree to a truce so that the Partisans could eliminate the Četniks, Tito would fight with the Axis to repel the anticipated Allied invasion of Yugoslavia. Hitler rejected this offer contemptuously, and ordered an offensive against the Partisans that almost wiped them out.

The war in Yugoslavia quickly escalated into one of the bloodiest civil wars in European history. The Partisans and the Četniks vied with each other to commit appalling atrocities and massacres. As the eventual winners, the Partisans were able to conceal their own war crimes, while publicising those of the Četniks.

Yugoslavia was finally 'liberated' with the assistance of the Red Army, sent by Stalin to crush and slaughter the Četniks in Serbia, and the naive support of the British forces, who sent tens of thousands of captured Croats and Slovenes back into Yugoslavia to be massacred by the Communists. The mass executions carried out by the Communists during and after the war are not nearly as well known as those of the Ustaše and the Četniks, but they were on the same massive scale. They used a macabre arithmetic similar to that of the Nazis. All anti-communists were deemed to be traitors, and ten 'traitors' were killed for every Partisan death. In all, over 1.2 million Yugoslavs died between 1941 and 1946, most of them killed by their fellow countrymen.

Their revolution successful, the Communists proceeded to impose an iron control on the state and its peoples. With the suppression of free speech, no public debate or resolution of the horrors of the civil war was permitted. The trauma was never exorcised from the collective psyche of the people, but was simply frozen until the collapse of the Communist system allowed all the old hatreds to spring forth again. The atrocities of today are the result.

Many books have been written about Tito's Communist regime, and historians disagree about many of its aspects. A short summary, included in the Appendix, is all that is possible within the scope of this book. For the moment, we will simply say that Tito exploited the 'nationalities question' by playing the different groups off against each other. This was essential to the Communists, who retained power only through the use of force and had to ensure that their captive peoples would not combine forces against them. It certainly aggravated the antagonisms that already existed, and contributed to the breakup of the country. With respect to the Serbs, Tito tried to strike a balance between a relatively weak Serbia and strong autonomous republics. To compensate the Serbs, they were given strong representation in the republics' governments. This included the key functions of police and military. The JNA's officer corps was 70% Serbian, the other ranks being made up of conscripts from all over the country.

Tito was able to keep Yugoslavia together while he lived. After his death, the incredibly complex structure of collective presidency, party committees, quotas and vetos which he created to rule the country without him struggled on for a few years. The Yugoslav economy was collapsing. The death of Soviet Communism removed the last support that was propping up the Yugoslav state. The Serbs saw their 'Greater Serbia' slipping out of their hands. The role of the army in a Communist country carries both power and prestige, and the JNA was not eager to see its privileges reduced.

Slovenia's declaration of independence in 1991, and its subsequent takeover of the border posts at the frontier with Austria provided the pretext to unleash the military in a futile attept to keep the country together by force. The horrors that followed can be best understood as a continuation of the long-suppressed civil war. What the future holds for the South Slavs cannot be predicted.

6

Friends
in
Need

Every day the news brings more reports of massacres and atrocities in Bosnia. People around the world, disillusioned at the abject failure of their governments to stop the slaughter, have come forward to help the victims of the war. Two of these are Dr Denis Rutovitz, a scientist involved in medical research, and Dr Jeanne Bell, a pathologist with an Edinburgh hospital. They founded a private relief agency called Edinburgh Direct Aid to Bosnia-Hercegovina and Croatia (EDA). Denis's motives for starting EDA go back to his early childhood, as he tells in the following account.

'*My introduction to real evil in the world was a newspaper description of a cattle train packed with men, women and children, finding its way slowly through a hot central European plain in the summer of 1938, to one of the infamous destinations later so familiar – Dachau or Auschwitz or Ravensbruck. Interminably shunted from siding to siding to give way to trains of more importance, its precious human cargo was held of no consequence at all. Now and again a railwayman, or villager, hearing cries for water, would turn, puzzled, then aghast, then try to help – to be curtly repulsed and threatened by the accompanying armed guards.*

The people on the train were, it seemed, Jewish, as am I, which probably accounted for the horrified fascination with which I followed that and other terrible stories of the time: but I do not recall that my sense of outrage, shame, fear, horror was related to that fact that I was of the same stock. I just hadn't appreciated that people could be treated like that. Most of the world didn't seem overly concerned at the time. It took World War II and the 1945 pictures of the heaps of starved corpses and walking dead in those camps to really awake the world to what had been happening. The world did wake up at that time; and it created the United Nations Organisation, with a charter imbued with hope for the weak, deterrence for aggression, rejection of the ideology of race hate and racial oppression.

In the summer of 1992, Maggie O'Kane published an account in the Guardian *of how she had tracked reports from village to village, of a cattle train wending its way slowly through the burning heat of a Bosnian summer. Wherever the train stopped people had heard the cries of women and children, and whoever tried to bring water was threatened or beaten by armed guards travelling with the train. No doubt because of the parallel with horrors remembered from childhood, and also because of Maggie O'Kane's careful checking of the evidence, this story disturbed my thoughts and dreams for days, more than anything else I had read so far. And brought home to me that the rapes and the burnings and the killings and the beatings and the mass expulsions were real, current, not in a far off place, but here, in Europe – in parts like so many others I know already from happier, holiday times. That the evil ideology of the Holocaust was back with us again, rampant, in places touched by the Holocaust itself, albeit that in the eyes of their tormentors the victims bore different tags.*

Jeanne and I were due to go on holiday in September – the month after Maggie O'Kane's story appeared. The thought of enjoying ourselves on a Mediterranean holiday ramble in the hills of Crete, just a few hundred miles from the horrors of the hills of Bosnia, had now become insupportable. By chance we read of a man called Tony Budell, who regularly drove down from Canterbury to Croatia, delivering what he could carry in a car and trailer to refugee centres around Zagreb and Rijeka. We phoned: yes, of course we might join him. Just two weeks later, Lothian Regions had loaned us a trailer; Miller Homes had come up with a minibus; Shaun Gillanders and Deborah Miller were coming with us in the minibus; and Deborah's fourteen year old son Calum had got his whole school collecting, and had raised £1260 and 1000 blankets. And Edinburgh Direct Aid's first convoy was launched. Rev. Andrew McLellan, Minister of St. Andrews and St. Georges Church, led his congregation out on the pavement at the end of the Sunday service, to give us a moving send-off.

Jeanne and I returned home after delivering what we had brought to refugees, and also to the wrecked hospital in the Croatian town of Lipic, devastatingly washed over by war and atrocity. But although one third of Croatian territory was now in Serbian hands, in Croatia the war had come and gone; we knew that in Bosnia it continued with even greater savagery. We knew also, even more surely than before, that we could not stand indifferently by while a new holocaust swept away a small people. We would go again, would raise what support we could, would do what other small things we could; and next time we would go to Bosnia. And at Christmas, we would go to Sarajevo – if we could – and celebrate Christmas in the beseiged city.

In Edinburgh and nearby, support continued to gather. Edinburgh Direct Aid was formally constituted. Rev. Andrew McLellan, Norman Irons, Lord Provost of Edinburgh, and Scottish MPs of all parties – Alistair Darling, Lord James Douglas-Hamilton and Sir David Steel – agreed to act as patrons. In October, equipped with two 7 ½ ton vans this time, EDA set off for Split and Bosnia. The party comprised Tom Bee, Chris Ruckley, Seb Rose and myself. Chris was the first EDA woman driver to startle the locals by piloting a truck, with much aplomb, over the roughest and toughest of roads into Bosnia – Christine was later to continue that tradition.

On Christmas Day of 1992, Archbishop Vinko Pulic preached a sermon in the cathedral of Sarajevo. The cathedral overflowed, with several thousands of Sarajevo's citizens: Catholic and Moslem and half Catholic and half Muslim and some Serbs and some Jews and twelve Scots from Edinburgh whose number included Protestants and non-believers and elders of the Church of Scotland. All the people of that extraordinary mix of races and creeds were there in witness to Christ's teaching that one should love one's neighbour. Unfortunately, outside the cathedral, across the river and all around the broken town, other men prepared their bullets and their mortar bombs and were soon to show again that they preferred to kill their neighbour and their neighbour's children, burn his house and rape his wife and daughters.

At Tarcin, about 40 km from Sarajevo, we met a fourteen year old girl, Sobina Avdibegovic, who told how just two weeks before, her house in Visegrad in a Serb-occupied part of Bosnia had been surrounded by armed men, the windows boarded up, grenades thrown in. The soldiers laughed while her family burned; she escaped by a miracle, rolling out the back door, then walked ten days over icy mountain trails to reach Tarcin. Even as she spoke, mortar and artillery shells were pounding down a few kilometres away.'

While Bosnia and Croatia were burning, the problems were also spilling over into the southern parts of former Yugoslavia. Kosovo, with its Albanian Muslim majority, had been made an autonomous province under the Tito regime, but the collapse of Yugoslavia brought it back under the direct control of the Serbian government in Belgrade. The Serbs hate and fear the Kosovo Muslims. The following letter from an official of the Yugoslav (i.e. Serbian) Embassy in Mexico City, published in the *Christian Science Monitor* under the heading 'Hatred Runs Deep in Kosovo', gives some insight into their reasons:

'After World War II, the Communist dictator Marshal Tito was always particularly interested in weakening the position of the Serbs. He decreed that all the Serbian nationals who fled the Albanian occupation in Kosovo were not allowed to go to their homes after the war. In order to trade with the Communist-Muslim leaders and to further debilitate Serbs, Tito in 1970 granted semi-autonomous rule to the Kosovo region.

In 1389 at Kosovo Field, Ottoman Turks defeated Serbs and their allies, who were defending Europe from impending invasion. The invaded Serbian lands were

Sheena, Halim and baby Linje, around 1964

under Turkish rule for 450 years. When the Serbs finally got the Turks out, they decided then that they would rather fight and die than live again in a Muslim state. The Serbs have the same feeling today.'

The restored Serbian rule in Kosovo has been harsh and oppressive. Early in 1993, Christine heard from her friend Sheena, still living in Kosovo. She was distraught. Her husband, Halim, had been imprisoned by the Serbian authorities. She didn't know if she would ever see him again.

Christine, in her typical way, decided that 'somebody ought to *do* something!' Ian and Averil McHaffie, fellow members of the Edinburgh Christadelphian church, were involved with EDA. Christine went along to one of EDA's publicity meetings, hoping for advice on how to help Sheena and her husband.

Christine soon realised that there was nothing she could do to help her friend in Kosovo. By working with EDA, however, she could at least do something to alleviate the sufferings of other Yugoslavs. Initially, she and Alan threw themselves into helping with the packing and sorting of donations of food, clothing and toiletries. As she got to know the EDA group better, she realised that the key problem was finding people to drive the heavy lorries used to deliver the relief supplies to Bosnia. Drivers with Heavy Goods Vehicle (HGV) licences were in short supply. Prior to his retirement, Alan had driven a rural library van for the Lanarkshire County Library and had an HGV licence. Less than a month later, Christine and Alan were heading down the A1 en route for Bosnia. The next chapter will tell that story in full, as Christine recorded it in her journal.

To help the reader to follow the events described in the journal, it is worth reviewing briefly the situation in Slovenia, Croatia and Bosnia by the time Christine and Alan made their two trips with EDA.

Slovenia was at peace, but was having to deal with an influx of refugees from other parts of former Yugoslavia. The Austrian government, reluctant to open its borders to large numbers of displaced Yugoslavs, was providing funds to feed, house and clothe the refugees in Slovenia.

In Croatia, the fighting had stopped, but there were still large numbers of Serbs in three areas of the country. United Nations peace-keeping forces had been deployed to ensure that the Serb minority would not be victimised by the Croats. The JNA had been withdrawn to Serbia. There were still many checkpoints along the highways and at the entrances to cities. In general, things were tense but not too threatening, although there was an understandable suspicion that the aid being carried might be destined for the hated Serbs.

In Bosnia, things were much worse. The three groups, Croats, Muslims and Serbs, were much more thoroughly mixed than in Croatia, so there was much more risk of snipers, shelling or full scale assault. The combatants in the areas visited during the March trip were mostly Croats and Muslims. In the June trip, once they had passed Kiseljak, they were into Serb-occupied territory, and the level of violence and risk was correspondingly greater.

7

To Bosnia and Back

The little convoy of two trucks left Edinburgh on the morning of Sunday, 7th March 1993, and drove southwards on the A1. In addition to Christine and Alan, the crew included Richard Spry, a first class honours graduate in English working as a barman in Leith, Jim Burns, a freelance journalist and ex-paratrooper, and Mick Cosgrove, a jack-of-all-trades whose main claim to fame was that he once painted the outside of Princess Margaret's house. Their route was to take them by ferry from Hull to Rotterdam, from where they would make a brief detour to Tiel to pick up the sixth crew member, Marieka Dwaarshuis, a young Dutch woman with a law degree and an HGV licence. From Tiel, they would continue on through Germany and Austria to Slovenia, follow the beautiful Dalmatian coastline of Croatia to Split, and finally head east up into the mountains of Bosnia-Hercegovina.

Before noon both vehicles were already in trouble, one stripping a tyre tread, the other with a puncture. Although both were quickly repaired, the delays caused them to miss that day's ferry sailing to Rotterdam. The extra day in Hull was spent getting the trucks weighed – the Halley, a 17 ton Renault moving van loaned to EDA by Halley Transport, weighed in at 16760 kg, the $7^{1}/_{2}$ ton Bedford TL at 8580 kg – and practising putting snow chains on both vehicles, as only Alan and Christine had seen this done, and from weather reports it seemed as though the skill might be needed. Preparations for boarding the ferry gave Christine the first of many new experiences. The remainder of this chapter is taken directly from her journal.

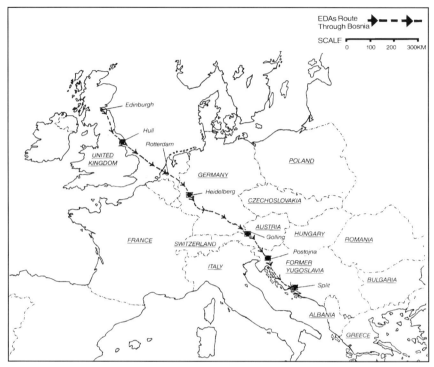

EDAs Route
Through Bosnia

SCALE
0   100   200   300KM

The route used by EDA from Edinburgh to Split

'I soon began my initiation into what was meant by being a lorry driver's mate (the marriage service said nothing of this!), waiting in endless queues with very large lorry drivers to obtain the necessary pieces of paper without which one can proceed no further. We watched with fascination and admiration the amazing skill these drivers show in manoeuvring their massive trucks, some with equally huge trailers. They reverse them up steep ramps and into narrow spaces as easily as I might park my bicycle against a wall. Alan was a bit nervous about putting the Halley into position but managed very well. The ferry was comfortable and the night crossing a pleasant interlude before the real work started.

Tuesday, 9th March 1993. We disembarked in Rotterdam at 8.45 am next morning, collected the "T" forms from the freight office, filled both vehicles with diesel and began our attempt to meet up with Marieka at Tiel. Not for the last time on the trip, we missed a junction and involved ourselves in a long detour to get back on the route. This meant that we were late in arriving at Tiel, but fortunately she had waited. After a discussion with Marieka's father, we decided to use the E31 rather than the route which went to the north of Arnhem. It was a little more difficult as far as navigation went, but they reckoned it was the superior route, being more level and quieter till just north of Koln. Some distance further on when Marieka was driving, the Bedford went one way and we went another. Both parties subsequently insisted that the other had made the mistake. I imagine it's one of these mysteries which will never be solved!

We arrived in Heidelberg at around 9.00 pm, all by now pretty tired. This is probably why our first minor accident to a vehicle happened. Mick reversed back too fast and just touched the Halley hard enough to break a headlamp glass. We were given a generous gift of 1500 DM to help with the expenses of the trip. As it happened, we did need to dip quite far into this as the trip progressed. We were taken to the homes of three kind people who had agreed to accommodate us for the night. Alan and I went with Thomas Fink to his home in Edingen. He prepared us a traditional meal of pasta stuffed with a mixture of what seemed like ricotta cheese and spinach, fried with egg and served with green salad. We were hungry and it was very welcome.

Wednesday, 10th March 1993. An early rise was necessary the next morning. Thomas's little daughter insisted on getting up to meet us. I tried some of my pathetic German on her and she seemed to follow me pretty well.

It was cold when we got to the place where the vehicles had been garaged. All of a sudden it seemed that perhaps this was going to be too much for me. So many new and unfamiliar things to be remembered and such a long way ahead and, already, some of the friction between individuals in the group was beginning to show. However, we were committed to going on and there were no alternatives except, perhaps, to take the plane back from Heidelberg – and that was an option I certainly wasn't about to consider!

We left Heidelberg at 7.30 am having taken on board some plastic sacks of sheets and clothing which had been collected for us there. I believe Richard owes the City Council for a barrier he 'brushed' against. We didn't see it happen as we were ahead! The weather was superb as we drove down through some of the most beautiful scenery, made more lovely as the snow was still thick on the fields and the hills, though fortunately absent from the road surface. One hiccup occurred when my navigational skills suddenly deserted me and we found ourselves heading back the way we had come. This was just as we reached the Munich Ring Road. It wasn't too drastic an error and only entailed going a few miles back up the Augsburg road until it was possible to turn and come back on the other carriageway. We caught up with the others who were waiting in a layby and had no more problems till we reached the infamous Austrian Border.

The mountain scenery in this part of Germany is splendid. The road proceeds like a gigantic switchback of long, slow (in the heavily-laden Halley) uphills followed by swooping downhills where care is needed or the truck might run away from the driver. Marieka was well aware of the need for care and kept the speed well in check.

The border did not give us so many problems as others have had, largely because of Marieka's command of the language. But there is no doubt that the "system" of windows seems designed to confuse, rather than enlighten and it is all too easy to miss a station on the way and get sent ignominiously back to 'GO' without the necessary £200! It would certainly help if the people one is dealing with were friendly but it seems alien to the Austrian character to smile or be pleasant in any way. Jim, particularly, seemed to have picked out the nastiest one of all.

We decided to spend the night at Golling, some 20 km further on. Sadly, the self-service restaurant was closed and the other one seemed a bit up-market, so we elected to cook in the back of the Halley. This was not very easy as nothing seemed to be level and walking about on sacks full of potatoes is not particularly comfortable. Also, our gas cylinder ran out, Mick's ceased to work and in the end we all had to use Jim's. It was not the most elegant repast I've ever sat down to, but it filled a space.

Thursday, 11th March 1993. After a very cold night, an even colder morning followed. That began, as Marieka had predicted, at 5.30 am when all the other truck drivers started up their noisy engines and left. Eventually we all crawled out of our sleeping bags, had a quick wash and went into the self-service to have an exorbitantly expensive breakfast – for what it was – served by another 'po-faced' Austrian.

We left Golling behind us at 9.00 am on what was promising to be another lovely day. The road climbed steadily through spectacular mountains dissected by a series of road tunnels. At the end of one of these we picked up a young hitch hiker. He was a Czech student from Prague, heading for Villach to visit his girlfriend. He was perfectly nice, but we learned the lesson that you sometimes have to deviate from your route to drop off hitch hikers and this isn't too good an idea. We resolved in future not to pick them up.

The Austrian-Slovenian Border was no trouble and we were through in less than two hours. The hot sun and the fact that we hadn't so far to go, relaxed every one and the rest of the journey to Postojne passed pleasantly enough. We did notice that we had left the really good roads behind and that the small towns through which we passed did not look so well kept as those in Austria and Germany.

Postojne was reached by 4.00 pm. As we had been advised, a crowd soon gathered. Among them was Shaha, whose son Adnan is presently at school in Edinburgh. We arranged to go down to her house for coffee. I had presents for her and the school teacher, Mr Prijić, from Denis and Jeanne.

As we had been advised, a crowd soon gathered. I decided to get rid of some of the sweets I had brought from Edinburgh first. Big mistake! I was soon swamped by toddlers with outstretched hands – and by those much bigger than toddlers who really should not have been interested in lollies. The initial orderly line degenerated into a rabble and, though the tone of my voice did restore some semblance of order for a little while, only a command of the language would have done the whole job, and that I did not have. I've since learned that what I should have done was give the sweets to Mrs Prijić to distribute. One learns, at times, too late of such things. The rest of the sweets, I am sad to relate, were eaten by even bigger children, namely my fellow truck drivers, all of whom seemed to share a passion for such juvenile goodies as Jelly Babies and Marshmallows.

We had a long and interesting discussion with the teacher with the help of one of his pupils who spoke excellent English. The story we heard of their sufferings touched us greatly – and yet they are among the lucky ones, having their family together and safe and having, at least, an adequate roof over their heads. However one can't help thinking what it would be like to lose all one's precious personal possessions and having very little expectation that they would ever be restored. They were at pains to point out to us that they were not fundamentalist Muslims, in no way fanatical about their religion. In fact they were not even very sure that they were good Muslims. It seemed to us that they were Muslims in much the same way that most British people are Christians.

After some time we were invited to share a meal with them. We had intended to cook for ourselves but it seemed rude to refuse. The food, which was a traditional Bosnian dish of puff pastry, cheese and yoghurt was absolutely delicious and appeared as if by magic as there was no cooker that any of us could see in the house. The others had, meanwhile, been collected by Mick and all enjoyed the food though all of us felt guilty about taking from people who had so little. It was noticeable that the family themselves did not eat much and we felt pretty bad about this. I also felt upset that we had refused a meal from Adnan's mother and accepted it from someone else, especially when she came in later on. Still, I think we managed to explain adequately.

All these families have sad stories to tell. The schoolgirl who translated for us lived there with her brother. Her parents are still in Sarajevo and, as such, in constant danger of their lives. And yet, despite this they keep their sense of fun and their care and concern for others.

Marieka and I slept at Shaha's house and were made very comfortable. She gave up her own bed for one of us and the beds were prepared with impeccable white cotton sheets. We were almost too warm. Alan stayed at the Prijić's and was given a room to himself. Perhaps someone told them he snores! The others elected to stay with the trucks, partly, I think, for security reasons.

Friday, 12th March 1993. An early start had been decided, so 5.30 am found us having a quick breakfast of bread and jam and coffee, running up to wake the fellows (who were already up and "chittering" from the cold) and finally visiting the teacher and his family for coffee and English/German/Franglais sort of conversation – lots of goodwill, not too much comprehension. The road stretched out before us by 7.30 am, a winding, narrow road through woodland, reminiscent of the Trossachs. Marieka was driving, efficiently as always.

At this point a decision was taken that when we got to where the checkpoints started we should try not to have the two women in the one vehicle in case this caused some harrassment. I had not heard of there being a danger of this, but I suppose there's a first time for every unpleasant thing so I didn't put up too much resistance, though I thought it's ironic that it took this to cause a swopping round of the personnel in the trucks, something that Denis had advocated from the beginning but no-one so far had wanted to do.

It is probably obvious from all that has been written so far that I had not yet taken my turn to drive the Bedford. This was not really by choice, though I suppose had I been prepared to be obstreperous I could have insisted. But I was told the truck handled badly because of its load and was still sufficiently diffident about my abilities to drive it at all, especially with perfectionist Marieka watching, that I allowed myself to be persuaded to wait till the road back. Consequently I did not in any way take my fair load of the driving. I regret this on a number of counts. Another factor was that Richard wanted as much driving under his belt as possible before the really hairy stuff started and that was probably a more valid reason. We had received reports of deep snow on the mountain roads of Bosnia.

The border between Slovenia and Croatia was easily passed. People appeared friendly and interested in what we were doing. It was here I think that I noticed the first of many other Aid trucks we were to see that day and subsequently. The weather was glorious as we drove through the twisty streets of Rijeka. It's a fair sized city which I remember slightly from my first visit in the early sixties. I wasn't too impressed then, and I haven't really changed my opinion now.

The coast road southwards defies description. The sea is an incredible shade of turquoise and in it are set many islands of stark bare rock. The mountain slopes which crowd the sea are also grey and bare, and without the sunlight the scene might be full of menace. But the sun lifts and lightens everything and every corner of the winding road reveals another yet more magnificent view. It seemed a million miles away from the place we were headed for, where, if reports were true, it was still snowing hard.

We noticed an interesting piece of graffiti on a bridge: "BELFAST IRA". Seems you have to go a long way not to be reminded that there are problems at home as well.

By 1.30 pm we were heading down the very steep road to Pag Ferry. We bought our tickets and within the hour were on the ferry. A totally calm crossing brought us to the other side, the hamburger stalls and the most revolting toilets I have ever seen! This, as far as we were concerned, was the beginning of possible danger. The defensive (?) guns on the hilltop were obvious. We knew there were checkpoints ahead and only Mick had any experience of that. Everyone reacted to this in their own way. I can only speak for myself and say that while apprehensive of something unknown, I saw no reason to fall apart with fear, at least until there was something to be afraid of. I therefore kept cheerful as did Alan, and I was quite looking forward to a change of company when I climbed into the Bedford. Just my luck that I landed on Mick and Richard on one of their introspective days. The conversation was far from riveting – probably as most of it came from me. I can be guaranteed to produce at least fifty fatuous facts an hour without even stretching myself!!

At the time, I wrote, "Now we start the dangerous bit." That was at 3.00 pm. At 4.50, I wrote: "Dangerous it has not been. Boring? Yes!" Five minutes later we went through the first checkpoint at which we were stopped. The soldiers were a bit deadpan and did rather stare into the cab, but when Richard showed them the list of what we were carrying, he says they made appreciative noises. This was felt to be an optimistic sign.

Soon after this we saw our first shelled houses. For someone who has never known the effects of war, this is a shocking sight. At first there's a sick, almost prurient sense of excitement about this but gradually the realization takes over that damaged homes mean dead and perhaps dreadfully injured people who even if they escape with their lives may never recover from the scars on their souls. We saw houses which had been utterly obliterated – one with a shell hole six feet wide. Most buildings had been peppered with machine gun bullets as though some maniac had just driven along the road firing indiscriminately and with no thought for what he was doing and to whom. In the outskirts of Zadar we saw many houses demolished by heavy artillery fire, but that was done some time ago and the area appears to be quieter now.

The rest of the journey was somewhat tedious as darkness had fallen and with nothing to look at and tiredness creeping up on us, there was very little talking either. We reached Podstrama, on the far side of Split, at about 8.00 pm and, not really having eaten much all day, headed immediately for Pizza Mario. We ate and had a couple of beers. But I was worrying that we had been out of contact with Edinburgh for two days as all the socialising at Postojne had put all thoughts of telephoning out of my head. Mick agreed to walk with me down to see if the International Refugee Council (IRC) office was still open. It wasn't, so we walked back to the Pension Tamarisk, a guest house where we had booked rooms for the night.

We were most distressed to find that the landlady had prepared a meal for us. All of us had stuffed ourselves so full of pizza that we couldn't eat a bit. I apologised and explained to the best of my ability and, leaving Mike to speak to Denis when he phoned back, I ran up the road to the restaurant to let the others know what was happening. I don't suppose it was so bad. The landlady was paid anyway for the meal and probably got to eat it

The March route from Split to Vitez

herself. It didn't stop me worrying the subject to death, however, and driving everyone potty in the process. I admit it! I have my faults as well – but just little ones!

Everyone was very tired, and glad to be able to sleep in a bed again. In the morning, I found there was no power and had to wash in the dark.

Saturday, 13th March 1993. At breakfast time we reviewed our plans for the days ahead. We were soon approached by Todd Cleaver who was working with Mick's brother Ron for another aid group, Bosnian Disaster Appeal (BDA). They were taking a convoy up to Vitez the next day, and were prepared to have us tagging along. This was wonderful news, and better was in store as they said that we would be able to stay in the IRC house in Vitez. At that point I had forgotten that there was a tentative arrangement with the Cheshires that we might be accommodated within the army base at Vitez, albeit in a tent. Still, I think that we chose the more comfortable option and it was enjoyable getting to know the others at the house – and probably good for us to occasionally get away from the military atmosphere. But I'm getting ahead of my story.

The weather, even at this early hour of the morning, was hot. Alan and I elected to take the Bedford and drive into Split in an attempt to contact the Government Agency of Bosnia-Hercegovina, who were the people to see for passes to help one through the Muslim checkpoints. We were experiencing great difficulties making contact with people who had promised to help us in one way or another, and found this very frustrating. But the passes sounded important so we decided to give that one our best attempt.

Alan had not driven the Bedford before, and took some time to get used to the gearing. Struggling with them, we completely forgot about the checkpoint half way into Split. They waved us down, demanding our documents. Fortunately we had the T2 form and the gift certificate with us. Then they wanted the back open. A moment of panic passed when we found the padlock key on the ring. The first thing they spotted was the beer. A couple of cans fairly sweetened the atmosphere and we were soon on our way again.

The trip to Split was a waste of time. We never found the First of May Square or whatever its modern name is. The traffic was so heavy, parking so impossible, and the time of our departure for Metkovic so imminent that we gave up and started back to the guest house. At this point, one of the most dangerous incidents of the whole trip occurred. We came up a hill and found ourselves heading straight for an unlit road tunnel, with literally no idea where the light switches were. Disaster was only averted by following in the tail lights of the irate drivers who had screamed past us – shouting abuse at fools who parked without lights in tunnels. I kind of saw their point!

When we got back, the rest of the party were sitting in the warm sun of the terrace as though nothing had happened. It hadn't to them! They had been discussing possible options regarding the problems of driving restrictions in Germany and Austria for the road back and had decided that to spend an extra couple of days in Vitez, perhaps doing extra deliveries, made sense. Though it probably meant missing our concert on the 23rd, we agreed as it seemed to be a majority decision. I walked down to the IRC office to pick up some faxes. By the time I arrived back, it was time to leave for Metkovic.

I enjoyed the run and we had a pleasant time chatting with Mick, who was driving the Halley. The coastal route is amazingly beautiful. All of us felt it was an area to revisit if ever this awful war is over. Things certainly look more normal here. There are no signs of war damage and people are going about their normal business, working the fields, playing boules, waiting at bus stops, doing their washing. Everywhere you see old women in the traditional black clothing and black headscarf. Probably many of them are about my age.

Just before Metkovic there are several picturesque blue lakes edged with golden rushes – very pretty. This area looks pretty agricultural, as if the growing might be commercial rather than personal. They also seem to have little fishing ports along the edges. On arriving, we went straight to the IRC warehouse to find Steve Katlin to get our Croatian checkpoint passes. He wasn't there. He was on a plane back to America and no one else knew or cared about our passes. To say the least of it, I was very concerned that we were now apparently going off into dangerous terrain with no papers whatsoever, but there did not seem to be anything we could do. To return to Split would lose us a day and would also lose us the protection and expertise of BDA. The only decision seemed to be to go on and hope that we weren't going to need the passes. This fortunately turned out to be the case because of the input which the [British] army were prepared to make into our activities.

We spent the night on some waste ground near the warehouse. Comfort was provided by a huge fire in an oil drum. We cooked up on the tailgate of the Halley and spent the evening convivially enough over a few of Tennant's "buckshee" beers, going, for once, warm to bed in the truck. I was worried about the lack of passes, by the inability to telephone Edinburgh, but the rest seemed confident that BDA would get us through. I had to realize that I did not carry, singlehanded, the responsibility for this group. Decisions were made corporately.

Sunday, 14th March 1993. First call for breakfast was at 6.15 am, after a really comfortable night. The ground was glistening with a light frost and the air was chilly but the sun was already beginning to come up and the mist lifted quickly from the hill behind the town. It looked as though it was going to be another glorious day. Breakfast was *al fresco* on the tailgate of the lorry warmed by the embers of last night's fire which Mick had coaxed into life again. I sat for a while on the step of the warehouse trying to read but it was hard to concentrate. We were all listening for approaching vehicles. Instead, the air was filled with the sound of church bells. It seemed rather out of place in this slightly alien environment. But this was still Croatia and Croatia is a Christian country.

Our escorts soon arrived, and by 9.00 am we were bowling along the road in convoy. First two of the huge noisy ex-American Second World War MAM's (I believe they're called), now sprayed white to identify them as Aid, not Army vehicles, then the two of us, then another two MAM's. The news was that Mostar had been shelled the previous night. We were headed for Mostar!

I was wearing our only flak jacket. It had been lent by Mick's brother Ron. I was not happy with this, another arbitrary group decision, in the first place because it put Ron at risk and I would have felt dreadful if he had been shot when I was wearing his protection. Neither did I agree that I, as the second oldest of the party, having had a good share of an excellent life already, should save my skin at the expense of someone much younger. However, no argument was accepted and I gave in. It was actually a most cumbersome garment and, while it may give some slight protection from shrapnel, it is virtually useless against bullets. [Christine was wearing a flak jacket when she was fatally shot in Sarajevo.]

Our instructions were to slow at the checkpoints only to allow the driver of the first truck to speak to the soldiers and then to drive right through. At the first one, the guard let the first two go through then held up his hand for Alan to stop. By this time he had accelerated so hard that he couldn't have stopped, so he just shook his head and went through. No bullet in the back followed, I'm happy to say, and other checkpoints were passed in a similar way and with equal success.

We reached the town of Jablanica by midday after passing very rapidly through the shattered remains of Mostar. Any war damage which we had seen previously was insignificant in comparison with the devastation of this once gracious town with its pleasantly rural suburbs. What had not been shelled to near extinction had been finished off by outbreaks of so-called "ethnic cleansing" and the level of hate and distrust which can cause a man to do that to his neighbour is something very hard to grasp. Practically every building along the route was destroyed, factories were blackened ruins, every layby and patch of open ground was littered with debris and burned out cars. There was even a car up in a tree and a dead dog lay at the side of the road.

The people who are left, and there are many of them, have clearly preferred to take their chance there rather than become homeless refugees.

Marieka, Alan, Richard, Mick, Jim and Christine lunching at Jablanica, 14th March, 1993. This area was overrun about three days later

They live in the shattered remains of their houses or in shacks which are reminiscent of the cardboard shanty towns of Lima in Peru. But again, there are hopeful signs that folk have not altogether given up hope. They are digging and planting next year's, or rather next season's crops. Let's hope that by harvesting time there is peace. It would be nice to think so, but I fear it's an outside chance. It occurs to me now though it didn't at the time that here we saw no children lining the route, hoping for sweets from passing convoys. Come to think of it, we saw no children at all.

We stopped for lunch in Jablanica. It was very pleasant sitting in the sun. It was a popular restaurant and there were many locals there too. I decided that the least we could do was to pay for lunch for our BDA friends and this was done. The scenery in this area is fantastic. The road climbed for many miles through gorges flanked by sheer cliff walls, over several ruined bridges spanning rivers and lakes of curious greeny turquoise water and at times almost to the very summit of mountains by tight series of hairpin bends. The surrounding mountains were snow covered and perhaps promised more severe conditions ahead. At the top we were stopped and told that we would soon be going down into Gornji Vakuf. We were instructed to keep close and to move as fast as we could through the town. There had been much "ethnic cleansing" carried out there following the publication of the Vance Owen plan, and only the previous week a soldier had been seriously injured when he was hit by explosives, thrown by a child. Not a place to linger in. We zoomed down into the town, and in no time were in the outskirts at the other side, only to have to turn all the trucks and go back because one of the big American ones had a binding brake and would have to be left at the "Britbat" base. It was a bit of an anti-climax.

When we set off again, Marieka was driving the Halley. As far as we knew, we were taking the main road to Vitez. We were, therefore, a little surprised when a few hundred yards up the road our nice tarmac surface degenerated into a mud track, covered in some places with solid sheets of ice. Marieka was not pleased, feeling that we were, after all, being taken by one of the "short cut" mountain roads which we heard lots of most unpleasant stories about. With the trucks so heavily loaded, we didn't fancy our chances of getting over unscathed. We were, however, wrong. It was the main road and after a few minutes she started to enjoy the challenge of coping with a big unwieldy vehicle in very difficult circumstances – and getting by.

Had we but known it, this was a good road in comparison with some that were ahead of us, and had we ventured as far as Tuzla, we would have regarded the Gornji Vakuf road like a six lane motorway! Be that as it may, our good lunch was soon shaken down, and watching the Bedford with its low body and heavy load rocking alarmingly as it negotiated the numerous potholes – the series of small ones were the worst – made me rather glad that Richard had had so much practice on the way down. Both trucks survived the experience, and everything else they had to deal with in the next few days. All in all, initial fears about their reliability proved groundless, and in the end we believed in them totally.

On reaching Vitez, we were taken by Land Rover to two houses rented by IRC. We were to be split three and three, but Richard preferred to be with the other younger ones. He did not however tell Alan and me this, which gave rise to some confusion over the next couple of days. Being split between two houses was a bit of a nuisance at times because new information about changes of plan had always to be delivered verbally. This happened frequently, and there was not always time to pass the information on and confusion resulted. It goes without saying for anyone who has ever been in Bosnia, that the telephones don't work. Neither does the electricity or water, except for a very short time each day – and sometimes that comes in the middle of the night. It is very difficult to keep clothing and even oneself clean. Perhaps it's as well that candlelight hides a multitude of sins!'

During the February trip, EDA had met for the first time the British Forces voluntary aid effort in Bosnia, in the persons of Lt Dave Kelly and Sgt Major Hardcastle. EDA had three truckloads of food, toiletries, medical supplies, clothes and toys, and the Cheshires' men knew just where to take it. The army's aid liaison and aid volunteers were excellent to work with. They patrolled the region constantly and escorted the aid convoys. The medical team in Gornji Vakuf kept wall charts showing the number of inhabitants in each cluster of houses, in each hamlet, how much aid each required, and how much they had had. They were scrupulous in delivering proportionately equal shares to Muslim and to Croat. They could provide guides, interpreters, escorts if required, and finally, if too dangerous for EDA's own vehicles, they could transfer the loads to armoured personnel carriers and deliver them therein – which was in the end how it was done at Gornji Vakuf in February. In March, the EDA team was again greatly assisted by the Cheshire and Royal Irish Regiments.

'Shortly after arriving, we were taken down to the Army Mess to eat. It is accepted by the UN forces that Aid workers need a lot of support and one of the ways in which this is given is in free access to their catering. We were told at the end that they are actually a little short of food, so this generosity may not be able to continue, but we benefited greatly and the few pounds I lost on the trip would have been a lot more without this facility. We were queueing for our food when we were approached by one of the soldiers. He introduced himself as Steve Arthur (Sergeant Major), and said that he had been looking out for us. In fact, he had had someone looking for us in Split. It was not surprising that he had not been successful, as we had left for Metkovic by the time he had started looking.

Steve had a programme of deliveries sorted out for us, and had organised that we would have a military escort at all times. We thought that the others should hear the details too and Lawrence agreed to go and fetch them from the other IRC house. The plan sounded just what we were looking for, its only adverse point being that it meant waiting a day in order to fit in with the arrangements with the people in the villages. Everyone thought the plan was excellent. We then went for a quick drink in the bar, followed by another one in the officers' bar, a walk to the press office to let Denis know we were still alive, and then finally a very dark walk back to the houses. Someone must have had a sense of direction because we did make it back that night but it was a bit of a miracle as Vitez has no street lights and the usual power cut meant there were no house lights either. Finding our way into our room in a totally strange house in absolute darkness was a slightly hysterical business, and I'm sure we wakened everyone in the process.

Monday, 15th March 1993.   Alan and I rose early (I can't speak for the others) around 6.00 am, to find – surprise – there was no electricity and no water to wash or cook with. Lawrence took us to the Mess for breakfast then back to write a fax for Denis and finally down to get the Bedford to drive to UNHCR in Zenica for a meeting of the NGOs. NGO means Non-Governmental Organisations, groups like ours and Equilibre. Almost all these groups are known by initials and I think you would have to work quite hard to remember what all of them mean. It was interesting to listen to what others were doing and to hear of the problems which they were facing. It seemed to me that most, if not all, of these groups had workers based permanently in the area and also a variety of types of vehicles to suit whatever terrain they were covering or what they were transporting. I felt we were perhaps more limited in this respect. However, we were going to have the great help of the army escort, while they had to rely on being known and recognised by the people at check points.

Sitting waiting for Steve to come out afterwards, I thought I heard gunfire for the first time. I dismissed it as imagination at the time but it probably was. It was a sound we were to become quite used to and quite blase about. Snipers are a dangerous nuisance here, but the main problem to the relief groups in the area seems to be the hi-jacking of vehicles. Generally this takes place after dark and we were warned that it was definitely unwise to be out in a truck or a van after 6.00 pm. IRC had a Land Rover taken from them right outside the house they were staying in and they had previously lost another one containing a very large sum of cash in Deutsche Marks. Because of this, IRC were pulling out of Vitez altogether, closing down their warehouse and moving its contents anywhere but to Travnik, Novi Travnik, Bela or Vitez itself.

While we were in Zenica, the others in the group were re-organising the contents of the other truck in order, hopefully, to make it easier to distribute fairly the next day. After we got back, we met up with them and helped sort out the Bedford as well. It really is a difficult thing to get right, especially as

Alan and Christine about to board the APC for the trip to Kiseljak.
Inside British UNPROFOR base at Vitez

some boxes are buried so deep that you haven't a hope of reaching them till the truck is nearly empty. We stayed around after the others left to tidy up a bit and then walked up to the camp to see Steve about the next day. While we were there, we were lucky enough to be given the chance to go out in an APC, an armoured personnel carrier. This was going out to Kiseljak to pick up the mail and was leaving at 8.30 pm. Time slipped by so fast that it was soon time to go back down to the camp and we still had not informed the others of the arrangements for the next day's deliveries, but we thought that we were only going to be away for about an hour and a half, so there would be ample time to walk up later and talk to them.

At the camp, we soon met up with our companions and were strapped into the seat of the APC. The noise of the tracks on the road surface defies description. Even with ear plugs it was deafening, and coupled with the vibration of the vehicle, which at one point actually hit the kerb (we heard later) and felt as though it was going to turn over, it was not the most comfortable ride I've ever had. But it was a new experience, and, as such, was interesting. We shared the back with two young lads, one of whom had just finished his basic training and was immediately sent out to Bosnia. Quite a shock to the system, I fancy.

When we reached Kiseljak, there was more to come. The Danish soldier guarding the UN base was not amused to find civilians in an Army vehicle and was very reluctant to let us go inside. But the soldier who was with us told him that we were being taken to see his CO, and we were allowed through after we'd been checked with an electronic device to see if we were carrying weapons. It beeped rather noisily as he ran it past my anorak pocket. I was somewhat embarrassed when investigation revealed that I had a dessert spoon in my pocket!

The troops at Kiseljak are based in a rather nice hotel, so collecting the mail there is a rather desirable duty. The British soldiers manage to spend some time there on one pretext or another, and it makes a change from the much more spartan surroundings of the Vitez camp. It did, however cause us some trouble as it made us much later back than we had expected.

We climbed out of the APC and started to make our way in the usual pitch dark in the direction we thought the house was. We soon realized that we were quite lost, had to retrace our steps and ended up, rather ignominiously, having to be escorted along the road by an armed soldier. Couple of idiots and no mistake! Still it had been a good evening and once again we were impressed by how friendly and pleasant these young soldiers were. I expect it was nice having someone different to talk to, especially someone from home – even if they did all think we were crazy doing what we were doing. At times we agreed with them.

Tuesday, 16th March 1993. An early start was needed again for our 8.00 am departure. We alerted the others to the arrangements and everyone arrived in time. We were to be escorted by Captain Matthew Dundas Whateley and a group of seven volunteers from his command, including a Medical Colonel from Malta who had an Edinburgh wife. We were to go first to the small town of Zepče. We were warned that most of the people we would see would be in uniform but this did not mean anything sinister. These men were the husbands and fathers of the women and children who were the eventual destination of our cargo and it was definitely in their interests to see that the stuff was fairly shared out. We drove through Zenica and a good few miles further on through rather pretty riverside scenery, crossed a bridge and were soon in a small square surrounded by storage buildings – for want of a better term they could, I suppose, be called warehouses. I was taken, along with Jim, the Colonel and the Captain to meet the head man. Fortunately, we also had an interpreter, a girl from Travnik called Svetlana and she was able to explain to each what the other meant.

The formalities (including the inevitable coffee) over, we began to unload a third of the contents of the Halley into what appeared to be a very empty warehouse. If what was in there was their store of food, they did need the little we were able to leave. It looked a pitifully tiny stack of supplies, and I felt quite sad that we were not able to give more. We gave them boxes of food and toiletries, survival biscuit and some of the potatoes. The box of jumpers which I had brought from Overtown was left here and on the way out we saw groups of children who would certainly be glad of them. It is quite funny to think, though, that somewhere in Zepče there are three men wearing Wishaw Golf Club sweaters. I doubt if they'll be playing golf in them, Zepče being fairly near the Serbian front line and, according to Jim's information, likely to be overrun in the next "push". One can only hope that this is not true. We were helped a lot in the unloading of the truck by the soldiers. It would have been a much harder day and have taken much longer without their help.

From there, leaving Richard in charge of the Halley as it would not have negotiated the next stretch of road, we back-tracked a few miles and took a turn up a mountain track to Zeljezno Polje, a village with the most amazingly beautiful setting. We had with us one of the military men from Zepče. I gather that this was necessary as the village was very close to the front line and anyone not known would have been treated with great suspicion. As it was, we were all far from comfortable in this village. The people had turned out in force and the men were all heavily armed. I had been taking a few photos on the way up as the scenery was so beautiful but one of the men had obviously noticed me and attempted to relieve me of the film in my camera. Fortunately I persuaded him to let me keep it. I had realised that some of the people might not wish to be photographed but hadn't thought that there would be any reason not to photograph views . . . that is, unless I was an enemy spy.

Once again, I was introduced to the leading man of the village. I did not choose this "greatness"(!) but had it thrust upon me, which is to say that nobody else wanted the job so I got it by default. I tried to note what was going into the storeroom but it was moved so fast that I couldn't keep up. I did, however, manage to get the necessary signature and stamp on the form at the end. As to the level of need here, it is hard to evaluate. The people were shabby and children's shoes looked inadequate, but there were no bloated stomachs and stick-thin legs and arms such as you see in Somalia or Romania. But that is why we are taking aid to these people, in order to prevent the suffering which we have seen happen to countless hordes of helpless people over the years.

Bosnia is near enough for groups like ours to reach, so hopefully it will be possible to prevent instead of having to come in at a later stage and cure. That is not to say that there are not really hungry people in other more remote parts of the country – this is borne out by this week's television broadcasts showing the people of Srebrenica being evacuated by the UN and so desperate to get out that they risk their lives and that of their children to obtain a place on the trucks. Obviously the risk of staying is thought to be greater than the perils of the journey, crushed together in the back of an open lorry in sub-zero temperatures and over roads which, in our brief experience of the country and the terrain, we know to be dreadful.

After the unloading there was another invitation to coffee. I elected this time to stay with the truck, sat in the cab and organised my papers. I was

Christine's photograph of her 'little friend Mariba from Zeljezno Polje'

soon aware of being watched. Outside was a little girl who smiled and seemed friendly. I asked her if I could take a photo and she agreed. I had momentarily forgotten about the soldier, but fortunately he was not looking at that moment. I got down from the cab and tried to talk to her. Her name was Mariba and she was eleven years old. I told her my name, and found out that three of her friends were called Faza, Fatima and Halissa. Soon I had quite a crowd around me. I would have liked a picture but my nasty soldier was near and refused permission.

I felt that in this one small incident I had made a more meaningful contact with a real person than at any other time in the whole trip. I will never forget that little girl and, if she survives this war, she will probably remember Christine who came in the truck with the others and brought food from Scotland. Maybe it's not important to make this kind of contact. Maybe it's a piece of self indulgence to want to be more than a "delivery man". I don't know. Different people have differing needs and, if explored deeply enough, many of our motives may be false and flawed. Anyway, "my little girl" brought her mother over and gave me a present of a fruit filled pancake wrapped in a piece of paper. It was really delicious. I shared it with Marieka when she came back.

Others also had special reactions to this village and its people. Mick left the coffee ceremony when one of the soldiers chased some children from the window by cocking his rifle and threatening them with it. He felt such aggressive behaviour to such young children was quite out of place. Alan was made uneasy by the way the men, looking at the British soldiers' weapons, were soon in possession of most of them. He was also surprised to be warned away from the window because of the danger of snipers. We were all glad to leave this place. Perhaps when people live in fear of annihilation it is not surprising that they suspect and distrust all strangers. Probably it is a necessary survival mechanism.

We drove back down to the main road again and headed in the direction of Vitez for a few miles before crossing the river by a narrow bridge. Mick was driving, and we had a pretty wild ride along a very uneven track covered in places with a thick layer of ice or slush. People seemed poorer here and the homes were, in the main, quite small. We saw one family cutting wood from a fallen tree and another woman washing her clothes in the icy river. The village of Begov Han was entered over a really tight bridge. The Halley could not have crossed it and the Bedford had a bit of bother on the way out because of the angle.

There was a crowd of men and children again awaiting our arrival. They seemed friendly and welcoming. There was less traditional dress here and we saw no children wearing the headscarf and baggy trousers which nearly all had worn in the previous place. They indicated that Mick should reverse the truck over a grassy area to get it to the window through which it was to be unloaded. It got bogged down in the mud and I greatly feared for the clutch in the ensuing efforts to get it out. But it led, as before, a charmed life and eventually broke free. It was then driven round to the front of the building and reversed across to the window, where it was quickly unloaded – so quickly that I hadn't a hope of noting what came out. So much for trying to keep exact records. No chance. We had meant to leave the rest of the potatoes for Tešanj, but the people here asked if it was possible for us to let them have them. If they wanted them so much, we were happy to agree. The coffee routine followed and once again we were glad of the help of the interpreter, Svetlana. Without the language of the people one is so limited. The drive out with the empty truck rocketing from pothole to pothole was a little exciting! All the stuff on the dash kept flying up into the air. Finally we just let it lie where it fell.

Back in Zepče we picked up Richard and the Halley and set off for Tešanj. Before long, the metalled road became a narrow mud track which wound in tight hairpins through beautiful woodland. Each bend was on a little sideless bridge with a cliff face close to the left and steep drops to the right. The Halley with its length did not find this particularly easy. It was necessary to keep up a fair bit of speed to avoid being bogged down in the mud, but at the same time care has to be taken to avoid putting the back wheels over the edge or demolishing the bridge with them. On one occasion Alan could not avoid hitting the parapet and we watched it fall over into the gorge – just glad we weren't going with it! Under these conditions a few miles take quite a long time and it was already dark when we reached the top of the pass.

The soldiers at the checkpoint prevented us from continuing, telling us that the town was being shelled and we would have to wait until it was safe. Everyone got down and there was some fraternising among the soldiers, who seemed friendly. At last a police car arrived from the town and led us in.

Our destination was the hospital. It had been suggested that we drop the box of medicines here, but as it was necessary that these be received by an authorised person, the hospital director had to be flushed out to sign for them. How one does this sort of thing without experienced help, I do not know. But Captain D W seemed to know what was wanted and be able to bring it into effect with ease. He also had the mayor of the town sent for and the man in charge of the agricultural commune to which the potatoes were going.

The unloading of goods proceeded with speed, helped by some of the men who were standing around attracted by the appearance of the trucks. At least these people got a fair load of useful stuff – masses of biscuit and boxes and boxes of toiletries. I was given a very long list of medical needs by the director of the hospital. Steve Arthur later said that this is one of the best equipped hospitals in the area and what we were seeing may have been greed, not need. This is one of the difficulties of this game. (To quote the

Captain: "Bosnians always lie!") While we were working, we were hindered by a rather drunk man who was trying to persuade us to take him with us. He said he had a wife in Sarajevo (I think) and was wanting to see her, as they had been apart for three months. Unfortunately, even had he been sober, it would not have been feasible, but it was just another example of the heartbreak caused by such wars.

All of us were growing concerned about the gathering darkness, so when the offer to go round the hospital was made, it had to be reluctantly refused though Jim managed a quick trip round and was, I think, quite impressed by what he saw. Apparently as it is a front line hospital, they do quite a lot of pioneering surgery, similar to what occurs in the hospitals in Northern Ireland.

We had to drive even further out to deliver the potatoes. These had to be unloaded manually, and at the end of a long tiring day it was very hard work. But there were many people to share the work and it was soon done. We now had two empty trucks. It was obviously going to make driving back down the hairy mountain track a little bit easier, we thought. But we did not allow for the two huge tankers we were going to meet on a bend. With directions from the soldiers and a lot of careful maneouvring we succeeded in passing without mishap, only to meet, almost at the end of the rough part of the track, a large broken-down diesel lorry. We were told to extinguish our lights as we were presenting a rather nice target for the shells. It was even suggested that we might have to stay there all night. This was not an attractive prospect, especially as we could hear gunfire and see the tracers passing overhead. However, it turned out that the lorry had only run out of fuel and this was cured by a transfusion from the spare can carried by one of the Land Rovers. While we were waiting there, another truck had appeared. This was full of what looked like wounded soldiers. We travelled with it for the next few miles and hoped, rather selfishly, that its presence would not get us into trouble.

The camp at Vitez was reached by about 11.00 pm, where we had a very welcome meal in the mess. By the time we had finished, it was well after midnight. When we got back to the IRC house, we had been locked out and had to hammer the door to get in. Our host had to come out in his long underwear to open up for us. I'm not sure he was too pleased.

Wednesday, 17th March 1993. We had hoped to move some medical stuff to the WHO warehouse the next day, but this plan had to be changed so that we could have the Halley's steering seen to. It had been giving Alan some difficulty and we couldn't afford to take a chance on it as there were still many miles to cover before home was reached. So, the crack of dawn found us on our way to Zenica, where the Halley was quickly fixed at the UNHCR garage.

This afternoon we were scheduled to go to Gornji Vakuf to discuss a future shipment of relief supplies from Britain. The parents of Major

Tracey Clark, the Medical Officer at the base, had collected a shipment of baby foods and medical supplies which she hoped EDA could bring out to Gornji Vakuf on a future trip. Marieka had hoped to go along. I think the inactivity was getting to her. It affected us all. We felt that we had come all this way and ought to be filling each day with Aid activities, but circumstances beyond our control were preventing us from doing this. There was too much "Bosnia time" when nothing moved forward at all. I've asked myself many times whether we could have avoided these periods of wasted time. Accepting the premise that we could go nowhere without a military escort, they were inevitable. If these restrictions were unnecessary, it is difficult to see why we were told so strongly that they were. None of us were unduly timorous, but none of us wanted to have our trucks stolen. It might have been a bit difficult to explain why we had gone against expert advice. In this case, we acted for what seemed to be the best of reasons, and if we were wrong, I really don't think it could be proved so without any doubt. Circumstances change in Bosnia from minute to minute. What is safe today might very well be very foolhardy tomorrow.

If Denis had been there to take these tricky decisions with us, it might be that we would have taken more risks, but he wasn't and all of us were anxious to return to our homes and our families in one piece. Others before us had taken the risks – perhaps they had the passes we had not managed to get. Some of them had been all right and some had come to grief and lost everything. I still think we acted correctly and I think, though I can't say what they might say now that we are distanced from the decisions, that the others all concurred with what was done. In no way were our actions dictated by any one person, unless it was Steve Arthur who knew the score better than we did.

Unfortunately, the Land Rover in which we were travelling was full of packages of Aid which had been collected by the mother of one of the soldiers who was with us, and there would not have been room for anyone else. So Marieka had to be content with taking the Bedford for diesel instead.

As it happened, she missed a very, very boring afternoon. The most exciting part of it was the journey across the wicked Gornji Vakuf road being bumped up and down and thrown from side to side of the Land Rover – much, much worse than doing it in the Halley. When we arrived at the base, we discovered that there had been a very sad accident; a child had wandered onto a minefield and was very seriously injured. The Medical Officer was required at the scene. We would have to wait. This we did for the next four and a half hours.

The base at Gornji Vakuf is not at all comfortable; in truth it's a miserable cold barn of a place with nothing to do. It seemed churlish and unfeeling to complain in the circumstances, but it was a boring wait. The child who had been injured turned out to be a mentally subnormal youth of 21 who had, in fact, been killed. The incident provoked an outbreak of inter-racial violence in the town. It was thus not safe for us to go to the hospital as planned, which was why we had to wait. Following the incident, there was then a St Patrick's Day Parade, when the soldiers from the Irish Regiment were given shamrocks by the CO. This was combined with a memorial service for a young soldier who had committed suicide. Earlier we had been talking with the soldiers about the boy who had been seriously injured by shrapnel when explosives were thrown at him. The three incidents together brought home to me in a way which had not been really graphic before that this was a real war we were in the middle of and people really did suffer and die because of it. It brought *me* up short. While we were waiting, I wrote the following two paragraphs in my diary.

Everyone here thinks we are crazy being voluntarily in a war zone. I'm beginning to agree, though it's probably got a lot to do with being cold and bored! The Aid business in general, I don't know about. This is an unpleasant war, and sometimes it's hard to feel sympathy for the people involved, as none are guiltless in this conflict. We have not seen starvation, though we have seen some need. But the people here were always poor in the sense of the consumer goods we take for granted. Now they live on handouts from the West, and as one young soldier said, the material things they are given allow them to continue this stupid conflict. Each side blames the other and none are totally innocent. The children perhaps are guiltless, but they are growing up in a society where every man wears a uniform and carries a gun. What's that going to do to their image of the future?

Would I do this again? I don't know at the moment. I have misgivings over the value of our aid and about the money spent getting it here. The people to whom it is coming are often greedy and resentful, if they think one has been preferred to another. No one wants cringing gratitude, but normal appreciation would be nice.

Eventually Major Clark returned, and we were able to make the necessary arrangements for the collection of the goods she wanted EDA to transport out for her. This all took about ten minutes at the most, which bears out what I was saying earlier about Bosnia time. We had spent more than five hours waiting for a ten minute discussion and we still had the unpleasant prospect of the bumpy ride back across the lovely road to Vitez. *Thursday, 18th March 1993.* We had a long lie the next day – till at least 8.00 am. It made a pleasant change from 5.30 am. We ate cereal and milk in the kitchen of our house and enjoyed a chat before walking down to the press office to see if there was any answer to the fax I had sent to Denis the previous day. There was a fax for us, but it had apparently been addressed in a different way, and we nearly didn't get it. It appears that there was also another fax asking us to try and find out if Equilibre had managed to deliver some specialist medical equipment, including a computer, to the hospital at Sarajevo. The previous EDA convoy had had to abandon their attempt to get there because of the trouble at Kiseljak and had entrusted the stuff to this other group. When we got home, Denis said he had faxed us about it, but I have no memory of receiving such a fax or of anyone else saying anything about it. Perhaps it did come, but it was not known in the Press Office whom it was meant for. I hope that this is the case, because otherwise it makes me (or us) look rather careless and inefficient. I don't think I'd have missed something as important as that.

Alan and I spent the morning working about the Halley, tidying it up, cleaning the worst of the mud out of the cabin, where everything you touched made you filthy, and wiring together the parts of the vehicle which were falling apart. There were a good few of them! As we were working we noticed two tanks turning into the square opposite the cafe, just outside of the yard. We wondered what they were doing there, but just got on with our work. We learned later that a death threat had been made to the men from BDA because they were moving the goods out of the IRC warehouse and taking them to Zenica. This was being done as a result of the Mafia hijacking of the two IRC vehicles. BDA had reported the threat to the Army, who immediately came down with the tanks and pointed them at the "Mafia Cafe" indicating that if anyone was harmed, the cafe would be blown off the planet. We had been in the middle of all this drama and not even realized it!

There was always an uncomfortable feeling when working around the yard where the trucks were parked. There always seemed to be groups of men wandering across and staring at us and the vehicles, not always in a totally friendly way. We had been told that vehicles were often robbed and we felt these men were perhaps casing us to see what we had that was worth stealing. Some of them were armed with Kalashnikovs and that didn't add much to our feelings of security. Probably they were all just hoping we might give them some cigarettes. On one occasion, we had been asked directly for them and had complied with a request that they guard us well as a result of our generosity. Probably it was a bad idea. Marieka said it would just encourage them to expect bribes. She was probably right, though these two never asked again and we lost nothing from the trucks the whole time we were there. Who knows what the right thing is in these situations?

We had hoped to link up with the others when they came back from Zenica, but as the day wore on it seemed that once again there had been a minor foul up. The idea had been to load the baby foods for Gornji Vakuf that afternoon, so that we could make a really early start the next morning as we had to drive the whole way into Split. The warehouse closed at 4.00 pm, and by 3.15 pm it became clear that we were not going to be able to do this unless something happened soon. We decided to run the Halley up to the camp to see if we could find out what was happening. Alan misjudged the width of the roof of the gatehouse as he made his rather tight turn out of the gate and made a bit of a mess of the roof, as well as tearing the curtain wall of the Halley slightly.

We had no time to stop and went on up to the camp, where we learned that the others had gone to Travnik to the refugee centre there. It would have been nice to have gone there too, but they hadn't had time to make contact with us to arrange it. It transpired that we missed being very close to shelling by not going. Travnik was being hit while they were there. It was a very frightening experience for them and a little taste of what living in a war zone can do to your nerves. They were both impressed by the way the Centre was run. The woman who runs it is a very strong character who makes sure that things are done properly. Anyway, having found this out we went back down to the yard and arranged that we would be loaded first thing the next morning. The gatekeeper was still upset about his roof and it took the intervention of Michael in the IRC office to persuade him that it was nothing important in comparison with the fact that we had come all the way from Scotland to help his people. The person who was most happy about the incident was Marieka who was then the only one who hadn't damaged one of the vehicles (apart from Jim, who never drove one and me, who hardly did).

Friday, 19th March 1993. The morning dawned chilly and frosty, but with the promise of improving later. We were down at the Mess for breakfast really early, then loaded all our personal gear into the Bedford to take down to the Halley. When the warehouse opened, we immediately loaded the baby foods and dried milk and by 8.45 am were ready to roll. The Army was late and it was half past nine before we were away. I said goodbye to Vitez without any grief. Our time there had been interesting because it was a different way of life but it was not one that would satisfy me for long. I hadn't read a book or listened to any serious music in a fortnight. Although the surrounding country was undeniably beautiful, there was nowhere you could go to sit or walk without the feeling that you could be risking your life. One of the most wearing things was the difficulty of keeping clean. The passage of all the military vehicles created masses of dust, and as spring turns into summer with its more extreme heat, this is going to be an even bigger problem. Water supplies are pathetic, and sanitation non-existent. The threat of cholera is real.

The trucks pulled into the base at Gornji Vakuf and, with the help of some of the soldiers, the food was unloaded. There were no pallet lifters or forklifts so it all had to be man-handled. Once this was completed, our work in Bosnia was finished, and we could start heading home.

We had a bite of lunch, a quick discussion about routes and whether an escort was needed from this point. To have one we would have had to go out via Tomislavgrad by a road which made all others we'd been on look like German autobahns. It was a unanimous decision to go it alone. We looked around for Steve to say goodbye, but I guess he had already filed us as finished business and was off to the next project in his busy life. I hope we hadn't been too much of an irritation to him. He certainly had been an immense help to us.

The checkpoints on the way out gave us no problems. As we were empty, we simply drove up to the front of each queue and went through. It worked every time and it speeded the outward journey greatly. Passing through Mostar, the destruction seemed even worse than before. The utter devastation upset everyone – perhaps because the people who had died in these houses were now real people to us, not angels but ordinary living beings who were being called upon to suffer dreadfully for some obscure and abstract doctrines peddled by their leaders – men who had no thought for the chaos they had let loose on their country and little concern for the innocent men, women and children who were suffering because of it.

The drive up the coast road was uneventful and we arrived in Split at 6.00 pm. All of us except Mick had decided to sleep in the Pension Tamarisk, but first we went to Pizza Mario for another delicious meal. When we had checked in at Tamarisk, I phoned Denis to tell him the latest. It seemed that he was pleased with what we had done. That was nice to hear.

That night the Halley was broken into and Mick came and knocked us up at 3.00 am. There was nothing we could do but cover the broken window with plastic and go back to bed. The only things stolen were the CB radio and two jumpers of Marieka's. Mick had had quite a fright but no other harm had been done.

Saturday, 20th March 1993. So it was that we set out from Split for home with one window covered by a Bosnian black plastic bag held on with green Heidelberg sticky tape to match the stuff that was holding the piece of plastic over the damaged headlamp. So effective was this repair that it did not have to be re-taped till we reached the border on the way back from Hull.

Breakfast at the Pension had been a very pleasant affair. It was warm and sunny and the lady of the house served us on the terrace. The sea looked most inviting but was a little too chilly to tempt anyone into a swimsuit. I had made my phone call to the man we had to see about the delivery of sheets to Resnik Refugee Camp. Fortunately he spoke very good English and I was able to note directions which enabled us to find the place easily. Another advantage was that it was very near the airport and Jim had to go there to obtain his UN accreditation so that if he goes back to Bosnia at a later date paths will be smoothed for him.

Resnik is in an area north of Split which comprises seven villages each called Kastelle something. It is a very pretty area except for the ugly industrialisation nearby which was one of the legacies of Russian style communism. Josko Tadin, who runs the Refugee Camp was, I thought very positive in his attitude to the changes he hoped would be made when this war is finally over. It was clear that the future of the region lies in exploiting its potential as a tourist attraction and he felt that step one would be to restore it to its former beauty. The war in this part, he told us, had only lasted a week but the damage to the fabric of the building was considerable. The room that we were sitting in had walls which had been peppered with shrapnel. There was even a neat hole through the centre of one of the pictures – right in the middle of the beach.

We were told that the camp had 1,400 inhabitants, a mixture of Muslims, Serbs and Croats, mostly women and children but with some old men. All the young men were either dead or with the Army. The refugees came from all over the area and many were from parts of Bosnia. Suggestions had been made that some should be relocated elsewhere, perhaps in more congenial surroundings, but the majority of the people, feeling that they now belonged to a community here, preferred to stay till the fighting was over and they could return to the homes they had fled from.

Life in the camp had improved since the weather had warmed up. Prior to that, because of the power shortage, the chalets had been without electricity for most of the day and people were often very cold. Washing clothing was also a difficulty and the toilet facilities were totally inadequate for the number of people using them.

I asked him what sort of help they were receiving from outside agencies. He replied that they had been given some flour by the UN and they had given this to their own bakers who had made it into bread for the refugees. Other than that, they had had boxes delivered by "Feed the Children", but the boxes had not been labelled and it had not been easy to distribute them fairly – people seemed to have grabbed whole boxes and then thrown away what they did not want. It seemed to me that better organisation could have avoided that, but after my experience with the sweets, I could appreciate the difficulties a little more.

Resnik is also partially funded by the Croatian Government, but this too has its minus points. The Camp organisers have to carry out the improvements and then claim the money back from the Government. Inflation is so high that by the time the money is refunded, it is only worth about a third of what was spent. I was embarrassed by the pathetic contribution of the few bags of sheets. Happily, I think that is going to be remedied by the next convoy as many more sheets have since been collected.

While Alan and I were in talking to Mr Tadin, Marieka had been sitting down by the sea reading. We joined her, but as she seemed to want to be on her own, I moved off to another part of the foreshore and dipped my feet in the sea. Alan thought that he was going to have a swim and even stripped to his trunks but the water was too cold and he had to give in and get dressed again. While we were doing this, we could hear quite clearly not too far from us, the sound of shelling. The news of the previous day had said that there had been heavy shelling in the Sibenik area. We were all too conscious that in half an hour's time we would be driving straight through that area and that we had no alternative to this route. Perhaps my phone call to Julie, saying that she could stop worrying as we were now totally out of danger, had been a little premature. It would be a very unkind twist of fate if we were to run into problems now.

This is what I wrote in my diary as we passed along that coast:

It is 1.40 pm and we are driving like Jehu along the coast road not knowing whether we are imminently going to be shot to pieces. It's exhilarating in a nasty kind of way, but all of us are coping by our own methods. Alan is concentrating on his driving. He is throwing the ageing Halley round the bends as though it was a Ferrari, trying to keep up with the pace being set by Richard, ahead of us in the Bedford. Marieka is listening to music on the headphones and has not spoken in the past hour. I, as usual, am scribbling, thinking that a shell would certainly answer the problem of what to do with the rest of my life!

Despite our fears, we made it to Pag without mishap. It appears that we had been misinformed, or that the dangers had not been anything like so severe as they had seemed. It was fairly quiet at Pag. I went to pay the ferry fares and was charged 55DM. We were all pretty hungry and treated ourselves to hamburgers and sandwiches before changing vehicles, at Marieka's request. The journey up the coast road was beautiful and there was a glorious red gold sunset over the islands before we reached Rijeka. Alan caught up with sleep on the back shelf. I thoroughly enjoyed chatting to Mick, hearing about his family, his Mum and his travels through the world. He knows and loves the Highlands of Scotland, a fact calculated to endear him to me, had I not already decided that he was a very nice man. The miles passed quickly and we had no problems on either border, though the Halley crew were stopped and searched for guns. Why they should have thought we were gun-running *out* of the country, is a little difficult to comprehend.

Postojne was reached at about 9.00 pm. Shaha made coffee for us and we talked to her with the help of the pretty schoolteacher from Travnik. It turned out that she knew one of the girls who had acted as interpreter for us, a girl called Susana who, we were told, had only had a year to do to complete her training as a doctor when the war interrupted her studies. The schoolteacher wanted to know if we could find out how to get her into Scotland. It was hard to tell her that there was very little hope of that in the present economic and political climate. We tried to see the Prijić family, but they were away at the other camp.

We had decided to drive on to the Austrian border before stopping, but some miles from Ljubljana Mick, who had been driving a bit fast for the Halley to keep up, took a wrong turning and the resultant furore meant that instead of going on we stopped for the night in the nearest car park. Alan and I slept for the first time in the back of the Halley, lying on pallets. It wasn't too bad – just a bit chilly. As we came north the weather did grow a bit colder but not so cold as it had been on the way down.

Sunday, 21st March 1993. Jim wakened us at 6.00 am the next morning by hammering on the back of the Halley – not because we were in a hurry to leave but because he was cold, not having taken his sleeping bag out of the back the night before. Relations were a bit strained, but during the day things got sorted out, probably better than they had been during much of the trip, and most ruffled feelings were smoothed. We had a lovely breakfast at a Rasthof just after the Austrian border and after that I got my first real chance to drive. I had no difficulties at all and really wished that I had insisted on doing more earlier in the trip. Still, I have to admit that pointing a truck along a motorway is not the hardest part of driving it and, if I am to claim experience as a truck driver, I must work at gaining more experience in town driving which is much more taxing.

The weather as we passed through Austria was lovely, and the fact that the pressure was over to a large extent allowed us to enjoy it. The mountains around here are in the region of 8,000 to 9,000 feet and are very rugged. We parked at a Park and Ride in the outskirts of Salzburg and took the trolley bus into the centre – all except Mick who preferred to do his own thing, as usual. Never one to go with the crowd. We had to stay in Austria until 10.00 pm, as German regulations do not allow commercial vehicles to drive there on Sundays before that time. Austrian rules prevent them from driving at all after 10 o'clock at night so one has to juggle times to keep within the law.

Salzburg on a Sunday is busy but far from lively. After much walking to try and find somewhere to sit and have a few beers in the sun, we finally settled for a rather nice place indoors. I don't know what this rather conservative establishment thought of our, by now, rather disreputable state of dress but they were polite enough to take our money and serve us. Refreshed, we went in search of (I can hardly believe this) a MacDonald's for our lunch. It had the advantage of being predictable and relatively cheap – which is about all that I can say for it. After lunch, Alan and I went for a lovely walk along the side of the river. Salzburg has good cycle tracks running along the side of the river next to pedestrian walkways and loads of people use them. The people dress rather formally and a bit dowdily, but perhaps that is only on Sundays. We caught the bus back to the car park where the trucks were. I was quite pleased to find that I could make people understand my German and that I was also able to follow what they said in reply. It makes it seem worth while trying to improve further.

Both trucks were liberally caked with Bosnia mud. As there was a hose in the parking place, Alan decided to wash the Halley, and Richard and Jim did the Bedford. Then I had to hose down the car park which was left thick with the said mud! When Marieka got back, she and Alan tried to get some sleep. I had a bit of a snooze too but later found out that I could have done with more, as Alan found it very hard to stay awake during his driving stint and I had to constantly talk to him to keep his attention from wandering and his eyes closing.

We drove up to the German border just before 10.00 pm, thinking that all we had to do was say that we were empty and drive through. Not so! We had to be weighed, get a Laufzettel (permit document) and then go into the corridor with the many windows and hope that we chose to queue at the correct one. We took the easiest course of action and woke Marieka, who once again proved her great value by getting us through in double quick time.

The plan was to drive all night. Alan took the first shift in the Halley and Mick drove the Bedford. At Augsburg, we stopped for coffee. It was very expensive for what it was. We paid about £12 for three coffees and a tea. Marieka drove after that. Alan went into the Bedford to get his head down, Richard and Jim were dossed down in the back of the Halley and I had my first chance to try out the mattress behind the driver's seat in the cab. It wasn't too bad, but it did seem a very bumpy road and there were many road works and a lot of traffic – an inevitable result of the driving regulations.

Monday, 22nd March 1993.   First light found us on the outskirts of Heidelberg at a service area called Hartwald, at which we stopped for breakfast. Lovely German bread and big mugs of coffee soon revived us, as did a good wash. Alan took the next stint of driving and Richard piloted the Bedford. We made excellent time, and when we stopped for fuel near Köln, Marieka took over again. She realized that Alan might have some problems with navigating through the complicated Ruhr region and also that when she left us at Arnhem, he would have to drive the rest of the way himself. Our next stop was on the Dutch border. The Bedford took Marieka into the centre of the town, while Alan and I waited on the outskirts. When they came back, we had only a short drive to the Europort at Rotterdam. On this part of the run, we met the first rain we had seen during the whole trip.

As we drove up the ramp onto the ferry, there were mixed feelings. We were all looking forward to a relaxing evening, good food, comfortable beds and, perhaps most of all, a hot shower. The rest of the way home, with the truck empty and the experience gained on the long road behind us, had to be a dawdle.

Tuesday, 23rd March 1993. Without any major hitches, we were soon on the dry land of Britain again. Mick was leaving us here to go back to London, his Mum and his kids. Richard and Jim took him into the centre of Hull for his bus and Alan and I set off on the way north. We reckoned that the Bedford would move faster than us and eventually catch us up, which it did, though much further on than we had expected. The sun was shining as we crossed the border, having passed the spot where we had our puncture on the way out and feeling that there was now a world of difference in the level of our experience. Starbank (EDA headquarters in Edinburgh) was reached at about half past four. We had been on the road for seventeen days altogether.

So what do I think about the whole experience now that it is over? We did what we were meant to do; that has to count for something. Everything we carried was taken to a place where it was needed and though we did not see starving people who were being saved from extinction because of our food we did see need and probably there was much more which was hidden from us because folk naturally put a brave face on things. I see the job which EDA does as more preventative than curative. No starving, emaciated children means that we and others like us are, so far, managing to avert disaster in a way which does not seem to have been possible in places like Somalia and Romania. I still have some misgivings about the huge amounts of money that are involved in sending out such a relatively small amount of aid but, realistically, probably no one can do it any cheaper and at least we have so far managed to get it through and it hasn't ended up lying around in storehouses while people go without.

From a personal point of view, the lack of real, meaningful contact with the people being helped is harder to accept. I would prefer to work in a situation where I could physically help – as in the case of nurses and doctors who went to troubled countries and gave of their talents and expertise. But I don't have these skills and to use my teaching skills I would have to have a knowledge of the language which I don't have and am unlikely ever to obtain. There have to be delivery men in a situation like this. That, perhaps is my natural role in this business and to want more is self importance.

Again, from a personal viewpoint, it was a learning experience. I found out that the habits which irritate my family also annoy other people and in the close knit atmosphere of a group such as ours was, people do not cover up and hide their feelings in the way that they might do in ordinary life. I was not alone in having character defects and annoying traits. The conflicts which can, in a short space of time, develop between ordinary men and women, is possibly a window on the sort of intellectual dissonance which gives rise to the kind of war which we were witnessing in Bosnia. There are no *real* differences between the Serbs, the Croats and the Muslims of Bosnia. What there is is a refusal to recognise this and a determination to persist in an attempt to control the ideas and actions of others and make them conform to an arbitrary pattern which the strongest group has invented. Naturally people will fight to resist this control just as each of us in the group struggled to keep our own individuality, even when it caused us anguish.'

8

Scottish Interlude

Christine and Alan's family and friends were very relieved that they had returned safely from Bosnia. In particular, Christine's mother Jessie had been beside herself with worry all the time they were away. Everyone hoped that they would not risk another trip, especially as the situation in Bosnia worsened rapidly during April and May. But both of them were now much more aware of the real need which EDA was trying to respond to, and they redoubled their fund-raising efforts, giving talks at churches and schools in Wishaw and Edinburgh. On one such occasion, Christine talked to a group of EDA volunteer fund-raisers in Colinton.

'I think it would be fair to say that Alan and I were pretty vague about what we were going to be doing when we set out from Edinburgh at 9 o'clock on a cold frosty March 7th this year. We became involved with EDA because I had a friend in Kosovo whose Muslim doctor husband had been imprisoned by the Serbian authorities. Thinking that we might get advice about how to help my friend, we went along to an EDA publicity meeting in February. It was mentioned that there was a need for HGV (heavy goods vehicle) drivers and Alan has an HGV licence. Less than a month later, we were heading down the A1 en route for Bosnia.

It's 1,800 miles from here to Split and elderly lorries don't go very fast. So the journey takes at least five days on the outward run and usually a little less on the return. Our route takes us via Hull to Rotterdam, Heidelberg, Salzburg and Postojna in Slovenia. Once reaching Rijeka on the Adriatic coast, we turn south along the beautiful Dalmatian Riviera, eventually reaching Split.

We were very lucky with the weather, despite how early in the year it was.

The nights were bitterly cold, especially in Austria where we slept in the trucks, but the days were bright and sunny, especially when we got down into Bosnia itself.

We were also lucky that, despite the distance covered and the horrendous Bosnian roads, we had only one slight problem with the 17 ton truck's steering and this was fixed by the UNHCR garage in Zenica. Mind you, we did return home with many parts held together with wire and sticky tape!

One of the things you notice when you get to Bosnia is that nearly all the Aid groups are happy to support and help each other. We were soon contacted in Split by drivers from Bosnia Disaster Appeal (BDA) who offered to drive in convoy with us to Vitez. They agreed to look after us if anything went wrong (e.g. mechanical breakdown) and this was a great comfort. Of the six of us, only one driver had been in Bosnia before, so we felt pretty inexperienced.

Nothing really can prepare you for the horrors of Mostar. You're driving along through pleasant rural scenery with distant views of snow capped mountains. It could almost be the A9 driving north, and suddenly you start to see building after building blasted to oblivion – roofless blackened shells, burned out cars, wrecked factories, some houses still smoking from last night's torching. There's a horrid sort of fascination – a kind of sick excitement – and then you realize that these ruins mean dead or injured people – parentless children – and you wonder at the reason why people – ordinary human beings like ourselves – can do this to each other, and for what?

Our destination was Vitez. At that time, it was a name very few people outside former Yugoslavia and the British Army knew of. Now, of course, it figures in almost every news bulletin as the site of the main British UN base and the centre of the Muslim-Croat conflict. When we were there, it was relatively peaceful. You could walk about the streets, even at night, fairly safely, though there was always the occasional burst of machine gun fire, single shots, or the dull thud of distant shelling to make you realize that your safety was pretty fragile.

To reach Vitez, we had travelled the now notorious Gornji-Vacuf road. We actually have a photograph taken of the fish farm where the Italian Aid workers were murdered. If we're honest, I think that's one section of the route on the next trip that we wish we could avoid, but there is no other way available. It's also a very bad road – unsurfaced, muddy, and full of potholes. It was bad in March and I don't expect it'll have improved much!

EDA is not an official UN-protected organisation, but, in practice, we could not have had more help and cooperation from the Cheshires at Vitez. Denis Rutovitz had advised them of our coming and they had a full programme of deliveries organized for us – all accompanied by military escort of two Land Rovers and eight soldiers. It had been pre-arranged with the head men of the villages. Without this groundwork, we could not have gained entry to the villages, which were sufficiently near the front line to make the inhabitants suspicious of all strangers.

If I'm honest, I was a little disappointed that the contact with the real people to whom we had brought the aid was as minimal as it was. I think I had visions of opening boxes and handing things out personally; in practice, this would never work and would usually degenerate into a rabble, everyone grabbing for what they could get. Those people are human and they have so little that need sometimes can become greed. So the way it works is that you must trust someone – usually a head man of a village – and he will see that the goods are fairly given out. At times this may be abused, but, as one soldier pointed out, "These are *their* wives and children. They are not going to deprive *them*".

We delivered our whole 17 tons in one extremely long hectic day. It started at 6.00 am and ended after midnight. Our first stop was Zepče, a small town quite close to Maglaj, where the Danish Aid workers were killed. We left the big truck there as it could not negotiate the narrow tracks to the next two places – Zeljezno Polje, a spectacularly pretty hill village where the predominantly Muslim population came out in force to meet us. Here, where the others went to have coffee, I made my only real contact, making friends with a little Muslim girl called Mariba and her sisters and friends.

The next place was Begov Han – a riverside village at the end of an incredibly awful track. There was a woman washing clothes in the icy river. Piped water is a bit of a luxury in many parts of Bosnia. The electricity only operates for a few hours a day and is often needed to pump the water – so people must make do.

Our final stop was Tešanj, a town only a couple of miles from the front line, constantly shelled and swelled to double its normal population by refugees. There's a hospital there, to which we delivered about 4 tons of supplies; this hospital is apparently doing pioneering surgery much like that done in Belfast – and for the same regrettable reason.

Beyond Tešanj we took our remaining load of potatoes – probably 3 tons or more – and delivered them to an agricultural cooperative who intended to sprout them and use them as seed potatoes. It's hard to imagine, the ways things have deteriorated, that they will have had peace to do so – but one can only hope.

Most of us in this country have been conditioned by what we see on TV to expect, in a country receiving international aid, to see starving children with big bellies and stick-thin legs and arms. At that time, we did not see anything as awful as that. But we were not in the worst areas – they are still inaccessible to groups like ours and often to UNHCR and Red Cross also. Also, unlike the African child whose misery is open to our eyes, the Bosnian child's body is hidden by clothing. So there may be a great deal of suffering which is not immediately visible. Until the recent troubles broke out, the aid effort, through the UN, was feeding around 400,000 and it was possible for vehicles to get through to most places. But the situation is now so much worse that the number requiring *all* the basic necessities of life has doubled, and the violence and banditry on the roads are making convoy passage much more difficult and dangerous.

It's also possible for people in this country to start to lose sympathy with the people. The image of a Croatian harridan swearing abuse at the frightened, beaten Muslim drivers, while shots ring out only a few yards away, does stick in the mind and you can find yourself asking whether these people are worth saving. But balance against that the fact that these women have possibly lost husbands, sons or fathers in this conflict. They have experienced fear which most of us hopefully will never have to deal with – for their own lives and particularly those of their children.

There are few winners in this kind of war and many many losers – innocent of any blame, wanting only to live at peace. These are the real sufferers and the reason why it is worth effort and a bit of danger for a short period in an attempt to bring them some relief – and, as EDA's mission statement says, "the knowledge that we are one with them". All that groups like EDA can do is affect things a tiny little bit. But there is no doubt in my mind that it is worth while doing.

One of the overnight stops on the way down is at a refugee camp in Postojna in Slovenia. It is full of refugees from all over Bosnia – people who have left behind all the material things which make our lives individual and pleasant. Until the last trip, no aid had been actually taken there. Yet each EDA group which goes is met with warmth and hospitality – the little they have they are happy to share – not for any gain, but because they appreciate the reasons why you have come – are happy to know that 2,000 miles away in Scotland are many people who care what happens to them and are trying to help.

From what I have been told, you, as a group, have made a wonderful effort here in Colinton. We are privileged to be able to carry this evidence of your care and concern with us when we leave on Saturday.

Most people ask us if we're afraid. The answer has to be that we are – as much for the anxiety of our families as for our own skins. But somehow the risks seem worthwhile – I just hope we are able to do *our* part well enough and that once again the "Pony Express" will get through!'

In a talk to the Edinburgh Christadelphian church, Christine defended the efforts of small relief groups to help the victims of the war.

'People have said to us, "Why go abroad with Aid? Plenty of people here need help." This is a fair point, but no-one who has watched the scenes from Vitez on the news during the past week could argue that the suffering is comparable.

The mass grave dug for the victims of the recent atrocities in Vitez was,

I think, in a field Alan I walked across on our way from the house where we stayed to the UN camp. I think I recognised one of the men comforting his wife as she wept by the graveside.

No one with human feelings can be untouched by such scenes. We must just thank God that we have so far been spared from experiences like these and pray that the peace we have enjoyed for the past forty years will continue and that peace will soon come for the suffering people of Bosnia.

But compassion alone is not enough – tears alone, no matter how sincerely shed, will not mend the wounds. In all honesty, there is probably nothing that can do that. The survivors of this dreadful war may never put behind them the horrors they have seen and experienced. The fact that many of these are children hardly bears thinking about.

In face of all this, it could be said that the work of a group like EDA is an irrelevance. How can a few cans or packets of food compensate for the loss of homes or loved ones? The answer is that they cannot – but, in giving them we are showing, in the only way available to most of us, that we care – that even 2,000 miles away we are thinking about their suffering and trying in a small way, but in love, to ease their pain.

This is a war which has been caused partly by man's inability to reconcile conflicting ideologies, of which religion is one aspect. We have not, it seems, yet learned the lesson that people of different races, creeds and colours need not use force to impose their ideas on others. From our point of view, our beliefs should direct us towards the breaking down of barriers and the healing of breaches, rather than the creation of more. What has been happening in Bosnia should be an object lesson to us all – in a personal sense, in close relationships, and in the wider sense in our relations with others. By trying to help in our own small way in Bosnia, we are trying to forge links and to show the love and concern for others which Jesus also showed. The parable of the Good Samaritan is one which everyone knows. The message which it sends to us is still as appropriate now as it ever was.

Jesus said:	"Which now of these three was neighbour unto him that fell amongst thieves?"
And he said:	"He that showed mercy on him".
Then said Jesus:	"Go and do thou likewise".'

By this time, Christine and Alan had decided that they would make one more trip to Bosnia with EDA. Deciding to miss the May convoy, they committed to participate in the June expedition, which was to go all the way through to Sarajevo. This gave them time for a few diversions. Alan rebuilt the small trailer which he used for collecting food and other supplies contributed to EDA by well-wishers. Christine worked happily in her garden, which rewarded her by producing its best crop of strawberries ever. She managed to fit in a week's cycling holiday in her beloved Highlands.

The birthdays of Jessie, Alistair and Elspeth's son Mark all fall into a five day period in the fourth week of May. Alistair came to Scotland for the celebrations. The main event was a happy family dinner in a Haddington restaurant beside the River Tyne, in honour of Jessie's eighty-seventh birthday.

Alistair and Christine spent some quiet time together, walking in the grounds of Châtellerault Castle and cycling in southeast Lanarkshire. Over a delicious lunch in the Nestlers Hotel in Newbigging, Alistair asked Christine when was the last time that they had cycled together. He was surprised when she answered: '1955 – the year we went youth hostelling in the Highlands, when I was fourteen!' Since Christine retired, they had been discussing the possibility of another Highland cycling tour together, but something had always happened to postpone it.

The final night before Alistair's return to Canada, EDA held a ceilidh for its volunteers in a hall in Edinburgh. Alistair, who had been taking Scottish

Cycling in the Highlands at Callakille, near Applecross. May, 1993

country dancing lessons in Vancouver, went along. The band looked rather an unlikely bunch to be playing this kind of music, and Alistair felt that they could best be described as a 'Celtic Rave Band'. Their enthusiasm was unmistakable, so much so that they played the Eightsome Reel sequence twice, leaving the older dancers literally 'reeling' at the end. Alistair and Christine danced most of the dances together, and socialised with the other EDA members in between. As he said goodbye to Christine that night, Alistair could not know that he would never see her alive again. But it was a wonderful night to remember.

During this period, the family had agreed that Jessie should not be told of Christine's and Alan's intention to return to Bosnia, in order to spare her unnecessary worry before the fact. The night before their departure, Christine wrote the following letter.

Dear Mum,

By the time you get this letter, you will have found out that Alan and I have deceived you and are, in fact, on our way to Bosnia again. I know that you'll be feeling hurt and upset that we didn't tell you, and wanted to write this letter to explain why we did it.

If you are honest with yourself you will know that from the moment you heard we had decided to go, you would have started to worry. You would have watched every newscast and read every scaremongering newspaper article and would have got yourself into an awful state agonising about what *might* be going to happen to us.

We wanted to avoid that and made a joint decision, with Elspeth, to keep you in the dark as long as possible. I'm afraid this meant telling a few untruths – like the one about going to St Andrews. We felt this was justified by the reason why we were doing it. That way we felt you would have at least the whole of next week – till Friday, when you usually phone – to live your life according to its usual calm pattern. If you had to be told on Friday, then there would be only a few more days till we would be quite safe again.

I'm sorry if you feel that we haven't treated you as an adult. We don't mean to do this. It's just that we will be able to do what we have to do much more easily knowing that you have not been distressed.

You knew that we had agreed to drive for Edinburgh Direct Aid on one more trip. We chose not to go on the May one, and felt that we could not refuse for this one. Apart from this, there is a real sense of wanting to do some good – to alleviate even a little of the suffering of the people who live with this dreadful war, not just for a few days but for every day of the week.

I honestly believe that nothing will happen to us. I've got a lot of life still to live and want to grow old with my family around me. There are thousands of Aid workers in Bosnia doing what we do and nothing happens to the vast number of them. I'm sure we'll be fine. I wouldn't go if I didn't believe that.

So, Mum, I'm sorry we didn't tell you but we did it for the best of motives. For the rest of our trip, try not to worry. You'll know as soon as we're safely back in Split. The drive home is a piece of cake!

We'll come and see you on our way home when we get back to Edinburgh – probably between the 3rd and 5th July.

Take care!
Lots of Love
Christine xx

For two weeks after Christine's and Alan's departure, Jessie remained unaware that they had returned to Bosnia. Eventually Christine's absence could not be covered up any longer. Elspeth was obliged to give the letter to her mother on Friday 2nd July, before the EDA party had reached Sarajevo.

9

Destination Sarajevo

It was Christine's practice to jot down in her diary abbreviated notes of daily events which she would later expand and transcribe into her journal. All the journal material quoted so far in this book was therefore edited by Christine after it was first recorded. Her last diary covers the final, fatal trip to Sarajevo. The sniper's bullet took her life before she had a chance to revise it. This chapter, therefore, is based on Christine's unedited notes, amplified by the eye witness accounts of Alan Witcutt, Brian Horne and Denis Rutowitz.

By the start of the June convoy, EDA was no longer at the bottom of the learning curve. They were better equipped in terms of flak jackets, helmets, radios and appropriate documentation than before. Led this time by Denis Rutowitz himself, the party also had an immense asset in the person of Colonel Claud Moir, one time Defence Attache in Belgrade, fluent in Serbo-Croat and chairman of the British Southern Slav Society. Claud's linguistic accomplishments and silver tongued negotiating skills proved invaluable in dealing with the many problems of passes, checkpoints and hostile militia groups met along the way.

Saturday, 19th June 1993. At approximately 9.30 am, three trucks left Edinburgh *en route* for Hull, where they were to catch the overnight ferry to Rotterdam. Alan, Peter Anderson and Stewart Kane piloted the Halley; Christine, Denis and Claud the Bedford TL; while Dave Hall, Paul Hardwick and Brian Horne made up the crew of the 'Bumble', a yellow and black ex-army Bedford MK 7.5/10 ton truck owned by Chris Chapman.

Brian, a journalist with the Edinburgh *Evening News,* described the departure scene:

'Friends and well-wishers all want their photographs taken with the team, everybody is extending their goodbyes, until you can't stand it any more – you just want to be on the road! You're really getting quite keyed up – what have I forgotten, what have I not done? – I'm usually "walking wounded" at that time because I've been up till goodness knows when the night before, trying to do all the things that I haven't done. As the trucks pull out, everyone's waving away – I noticed Dave Hall's daughter went away with a wee quiet tear in her eye! As soon as the trucks get around the corner and out of sight of the warehouse, it all goes quiet inside the trucks, and you've got that few moments of wondering "What are we doing now and where are we going?", until eventually the conversation starts to build up again, that kind of conversation of people who are getting to know each other – you know you're going to be living shoulder to shoulder for the next couple of weeks, and you've got all this kind of skirmishing around. Everybody's been waltzing around, putting on a brave show for the people who have come to see them off, and then the first time you realise what you're doing is when you know that you are really on the road now.'

The first day has a special element of stress, because missing the ferry wastes a whole day (as happened during the March trip). The team has not yet *become* a team.

Brian: 'Every time you pass a service station, someone else wants to fuel up. Nobody has yet got to the point that you all go for coffee together. You get that big sense of relief when you finally get loaded onto the ferry. As soon as you are on the ferry, you have a really good night, because you know that you're going to be looked after, you can't get lost, you've got a good meal, you've got nothing to do except put the food on your plate and eat it.'

Brian has made several trips with EDA, and is well aware that life is reduced to basics: food, shelter, somewhere to sleep, security from attack or robbery; all of these assume primary importance when you reach the war zone.

The drive down to Hull was uneventful. Alan commented on how passing drivers and bus passengers reacted to the signs on the EDA trucks. 'You could see either resentment or admiration on their faces. The reactions were a lot more positive than negative. The cars would toot their horns and give you a smile. There was one bus that passed us. By the time it had got past us, there was about a dozen passengers at the back window, waving furiously to us! Later, in Austria, two Dutch motor cyclists watched as we got out the flak jackets to try them on for size. They were full of praise, and very interested in what we were going to do.' The crew members found this kind of reaction a boost to their morale, but also rather embarrassing. Alan put it well: 'I was so proud at being humble!'

The ferry crossing was a big social occasion, which had the important effect of welding the disparate individual volunteers into a cohesive team.

Somebody produced a pack of cards and came up with a game called 'Switch', new to many of the party, which was a real ice-breaker. 'A couple of pints of lager, and playing cards till one o'clock in the morning – that was the big turn-round – after that we were a group.'

Sunday, 20th June 1993. The ferry docked at 8.00 am the next morning, in lovely, sunny weather. The team now faced a long, twelve hour day to get to Heidelberg. Christine noted in her diary:

'My first chance driving the TL – bit hairy coming out through Rotterdam but lucky because it was Sunday and quiet. Found handling quite difficult – tendency to swing and over-correct steering. Also quite hard to maintain steady speed. Improved gradually, but my gear changing is still pathetic and getting nervous doesn't help. Drove 276 km. Claud took over after lunch. At present, stuck 30 miles from Heidelberg with flat battery – no liquid in cells. Pity, we were doing so well. It's now 6.30 pm. Problem quickly solved and we're away again.

Reached Heidelberg around 7.00 pm. Hassle getting diesel in in-town gas station. Bit of lack of co-operation from irate German car owner who could have moved his car to help us, but preferred to watch us struggling, then abused us when the fellows moved his car over. Not too good for international relations, really.'

As on every EDA mission, the group were received with 'right royal' hospitality by Denis's friends at the Heidelberg cancer research hospital. The doctors and scientists there have raised substantial funds for EDA's Bosnian relief activity. They also provided medical and other supplies, including a sophisticated medical diagnostic instrument called a photospectrometer, which was taken to Split and then flown into Sarajevo on a United Nations aircraft. The team members were put up in pairs at the homes of the hospital staff. Brian was impressed to find that, in Heidelberg, crates of beer are delivered to homes and left on the street outside, just as milk is in Britain, and nobody steals it!

Monday, 21st June 1993. Brian remembers this morning as pretty chaotic. Paul had left his money belt in the car of one of the Germans, who had already gone to work.Once he had been tracked down, the trucks left in pouring rain, now an hour and a half late. Christine, who had slept at the home of Lea and Simon Thomas, commented on how well behaved their children were in comparison to British kids.

Once again, difficulties in navigating through the city wasted more time, as one of the trucks 'went on Cook's tour of Heidelberg'. As a British soldier later described it, they became 'temporarily topographically embarrassed'. These problems were the result of the confusing way that German autobahns are designed, using forks instead of roundabouts at exits, which demands local knowledge to avoid missing turnings.

Heidelberg is the last haven of comfort, peace and tranquillity on the journey to Bosnia. Now the trucks must leave behind the familiarity and security of the European Community. Whereas the border between the Netherlands and Germany is marked merely by a sign on the roadside, crossing into Austria is a frustrating process involving hours of delay, first clearing out of Germany, and then reversing the procedure to obtain admission to Austria. The world of frontiers and checkpoints begins here.

Around noon, an accident on the autobahn delayed the convoy for about two hours. Christine recorded:

'Travelling in Halley again. Some slight "aggro" developing about forcible moving from truck to truck. Bumble crew want to stay together and *be* a crew. Also some moans about time wasting at stops. Can see the point of this, though it's very pleasant to have a break.

The time lost in the traffic jam has made us behind schedule. We'll be pretty late getting to Golling. Apparently we may go on through the night to speed things up. The Halley drivers are beefing slightly about not having enough turns. But all this is so far pretty harmless. After last trip's experiences, I'm a bit nervous about "edge" developing, but the group does seem pretty well balanced.

We drove to an alternative (Austrian border) crossing at Freilassen, which was much quieter than the usual one. We still had a bit of a problem finding the correct windows in the correct order. A helpful border official, who was initially somewhat nit picking but latterly very pleasant, advised us of the order. The process took about an hour and was relatively painless, except when we thought the trucks had to be sealed and we would have to carry all personal stuff in the cabs. However, he finally said 'Es gar nichts gehr' and told us we could go. We arrived at Golling around 10.00 pm and organized a very pleasant *alfresco* cook up. The rain was off by this time, and it was pleasantly warm. We went to bed around 12.15 am, some in and some under the trucks. Good night – quite peaceful.'

Golling is simply a motorway pull-off, just over the border in Austria. It has a large parking area, an 'eatery' and a souvenir shop. Truckers are well provided for, with showers and extra facilities in the wash rooms. For the relief groups, this is the first time they are really thrown upon their own resources, having to open a tin, light a camp stove to cook a meal, or put out a sleeping bag under a truck to bed down for the night. They have to put up with the curiosity of other travellers, who stand and stare at them, unsure whether to say anything or not. The only other place to eat there is the Rasthof, a rather pretentious hostelry which made the group members all too aware of their dirty clothes and three day stubble.

Sleeping under the trucks was a new adventure for many of the party. Before deciding where to place the sleeping bags, it was important to check for oil leaks after the trucks had been parked for a while to avoid being dripped on during the night. Some people found it worthwhile sleeping next to Claud, in order to benefit when he brought out his hip flask for a nightcap.

Tuesday, 22nd June 1993. The fourth day of the expedition began with an apparent crisis. The mountain road from Golling to Salzburg is a masterpiece of highway engineering, levelled by an endless sequence of bridges and tunnels. As the trucks passed through the first (two mile long) tunnel, the Bumble spluttered and stopped. The other trucks stopped at the other end of the tunnel and waited worriedly for what seemed like a long time. Eventually the Bumble reappeared, and the convoy continued on its way. The problem had been self-inflicted. The crew had turned off the fuel supply, as a precaution to avoid theft of the vehicle, and had forgotten to turn it on again in the morning. Shortly after this, Christine wrote:

'Driving now towards Villach through glorious Alpine scenery. Weather is improving and it looks as though it may be hot later. 9.15 am now. Stopped for coffee at exorbitantly expensive Rasthof. Two coffees, two slices of cake cost 110 schillings – more than £10! Left there with me driving the TL. Managing much better.

Wonderful scenery, weather hotting up. Have changed into shorts, as I may choose not to wear them in Bosnia for the obvious reasons. Some muck up of gear-changing at border at Karavanke. Austrian side very smooth and quick, Slovenian side now being dealt with. I'm sitting on the kerb in the sun writing this. Looking forward to the challenge of the remaining drive.

5.35 pm: 10 km to go to Postojne. The challenge of the rest of the drive I did not enjoy. Suddenly my gear changing went to "pigs and whistles" and the more Denis commented, the worse I got. Just before Ljubljana, we made a diesel stop and changed drivers. My confidence is a bit wobbly. Some reorganization of the load was attempted – packages of shoes were sorted out and we also tried on flak jackets and helmets. A flak jacket costs £400, so they must be looked after. The heat now is really intense, and working on the load is pretty heavy going. Not that I did much. Alan in a grumbly mood, but everyone else seems cheery and positive. The last stretch through Ljubljana went smoothly – all trucks coping well with the long steep gradients. Stopped on outskirts of Postojne to dress more formally.'

At Postojne, the group again stayed at the refugee camp, originally a motel. Christine was excited to be back, as she had been told at the ceilidh that the Bosnian refugees she had met on the March trip had been asking about her and wanted to know if she was coming back. She had letters and presents to deliver to many of them. Everyone there called her Christina, attaching the feminine ending 'a' common in Slavic languages. Again, there was the difficulty of trying to say 'no' to offers of hospitality which the refugees could ill afford to provide, without giving offence. The solution was for some of the party to accept, while the rest stayed to guard the trucks, this being an area where theft was all too common. The camp is virtually without men, so Christine was always included in the 'hospitality' group. She wrote:

'Welcome from Prijić family, very warm as always. Ismet, Ramkha and their two sons are lovely people and young Leila has a really warm personality. Also met Shaha again. Was pleased to hear that Nahima was now in Germany. She has relations there and that helped her to get out. She says she'll write to me.

We had a meal with Ismet and Ramkha (Alan and me, Denis, Claud & Brian). They are so generous and kindly – can't do enough for us. It's a pleasure to be able to do little things in return. I wish some of the people who say "Muslim" with a curl of the lip could meet these wonderful people. Their situation is desperately depressive but they have such vitality and sense of fun.

An impromptu game of football started and some of the chaps joined in. Everyone was having fun and there was lots of laughter and good will generated. People wanted their children photographed and I got into conversation with several people, including a Croatian lady from Slavonski Brod and a family from Jajce with a subnormal son. The Croatian lady's grandson was called Damir. I spoke to her in German. I felt that many children looked less well cared for than the last time – some were shabby and one poor little soul was covered in sores. I hope all the pictures come out. If they do, it should be most useful for talks for the western press.

We had coffee with Ramkha and Ismet, and then Leila came with me to speak to Shaha. The young girls fairly fancied Brian. Passing aid workers *do* seem to make their lives more interesting. The conversation between them was obviously quite raunchy! Clearly these Muslim girls are not suppressed like their Islamic sisters. Once again, the laughter and fun of these people, who, in their desperate situation could be sunk in depression and misery, is quite amazing. As Denis said, it's hard to imagine how men can lob shells into the middle of such groups of happy people with the deliberate intention of killing and maiming.

We were persuaded into staying with the Prijićs and had a comfortable night, slightly spoiled by having to wake up by 5.00 am. One thing which all these people want is to be able to get word to their families who are still in Bosnia. We try to do this when we can and hope we'll be able.'

Brian discovered that a little knowledge of the language could be an embarrassing, if not dangerous, thing. His attempts to write down 'We are going to Sarajevo, with luck' were met with gales of laughter. Eventually one of the Muslim girls explained that what he had actually written meant 'We are going to a Sarajevo toilet'. This proved to be a rather prophetic statement.

Wednesday, 23rd June 1993. Leaving Postojne at 7.00 am the following morning, the party reached the Croatian border about 8.00 am, which was much busier than the previous time and took about an hour to get through. The next place of any size was the old industrial port city of Rijeka, known to the Italians as Fiume.

Brian described the coast road from Rijeka to Split: 'You have this superb Adriatic colour on one side, you've got these real harsh mountains that start up on the other side, you've got a grey "granitey" type rock, tiny little stunted plants clinging all over it – the sun's hammering down overhead.' As a result of the 1991 fighting in Croatia, the route has been diverted onto a tiny little back road on the island of Pag. On this segment, the expedition narrowly escaped disaster. Christine recorded in her diary:

'11.00 am – petrol station stop to make phone call to Split. Making pretty good time so far. Stopping for food at Pag. Weather very humid and overcast. Travelling with Peter and Paul in the Halley. Appalled, as before, by the hairy driving of the natives, we proceeded as fast as possible to Pag. Denis [is] being annoying about techniques of driving. Alan has now taken over for the short stretch to Pag. About half an hour to wait at ferry. Heat now considerable. Crossing and journey through Zadar and Sibenik fairly straightforward. Weather changed to very wet and thundery – beautiful rainbows.

About 40 km from Split, the Bumble spun off the road on some kind of slippery surface, perhaps caused by rain. It hit a pole, then bounced back into a crash barrier. Only this prevented it from falling 15 ft to the water below. Alan driving the Halley managed to avoid Bumble and braked only to be hit from behind by the Bedford TL driven by Stewart. What total carnage! Broken glass, steaming radiators and Dave and Brian bleeding from head and arm gashes. Paul had escaped miraculously unhurt. Talk about shooting yourself in the foot! We really had. In one brief second we had apparently wiped out, not only the project, but the three trucks as well.'

Alan described the moments leading up to the crash. 'I was second in the line, driving the Halley. Brian was driving the front truck. I kept watching the spray coming up from the rear wheels, and thinking it was very odd, because it looked like soapy water. It must have been a chemical leaching out of the dressing used on the road surface. It made it extremely slippery. While I was watching it, I suddenly felt the Halley starting to slide a wee bit at the front, so of course I immediately took my foot off the accelerator, but didn't touch the brakes. Then I felt the back starting to go round. I thought "Oh, this is really bad!", and just at that moment I saw the Bumble starting to spin.'

Brian had to make a quick decision:

'It was obvious that we were going to hit the embankment and the wall, so I thought "If it's going to hit it, let's hit it straight!", because the last thing I wanted to do was to run a wheel up and roll it. We banged into the bank, demolished a big road sign, demolished the inside of the cab – people flying around everywhere – and then the next thing I knew was we were just sliding back, with the sea growing ever larger in the mirrors, but luckily the brake system was still intact, the air brakes went on, and it stopped just after it had crunched through the barrier. The one clear memory that I have is thinking to myself "What a lot of arms and legs there are in this cab!" It was like one of these crazy old films about weightless astronauts.' (Seat belts are not required in commercial vehicles, but EDA will certainly fit them in future.)

Alan again:

'As they hit the wall, that blocked the road. I knew that I couldn't stop in the distance. As they gradually slid by, I saw a gap and just sneaked through it. Christine was already saying "If you stop here, I'll get out with the First Aid kit", so as I was slowing down just past the Bumble, Stewart was coming up behind me, and he walloped me one! It was too slippery for him to avoid hitting me. Eventually the police appeared, and we had to show our passports and driving licences. The road was stopped in both directions for a couple of hours.'

Christine wrote:

'I put emergency dressings on Brian's head and Dave's arm and cleaned up Paul who was only covered in blood but not bleeding. I was worried about Stewart who seemed unhurt but shocked, but once the ambulance had come to take Dave and Brian to the hospital at Marina (where they were patched up), I had to go and sit in the Halley, which we had parked well down the road with a warning triangle at the front. All the traffic was held up and we were a source of considerable amusement to passersby and irritation to the drivers who had to wait for the road to be cleared. Eventually, after much to-ing and fro-ing, we managed to move the Halley back up the road to the police station. We were then instructed to go to Trogir to the big police station and eventually joined there by the others and the two trucks which were driveable, though damaged.

Mr Ljubo Bosliković, the owner of the Pension Tamarisk (in Split) had brought a friend with a car to pick up the injured and Stewart, and it was decided I go too. The drive back in Mr B's car was pretty horrendous as he drove really, really fast and close to the people in front. Croatian drivers are crazy. As we came in, Yasminka was waiting for her husband, to say that she too had had a crash and their car was a total write off, having been hit in the side. Her husband was not happy and it was hard for her then to make a meal for nine people. However eventually the others arrived, and we sat down for our relatively (why did I say that?) really social meal.

Despite what had happened, there was friendliness, laughter and optimism, especially at the police station earlier when we met up again with a "repaired" Brian and Dave. Unfortunately, Alan and I were stuck with the Halley that night, Stewart took the TL and Brian the pod of the Bumble. I'm hoping to have a bed tonight, as I was not able to sleep very well because of the traffic.

Thursday, 24th June 1993. We were wakened at 6.00 am by the sounds of gun fire. After breakfast, we started to re-organise the loads in the vehicles. In the heat, it was very hard work, but by lunchtime it was done. Denis, Claud and Paul went off to see if they could find a garage to sort out our problems. Since then, it's been a bit of hanging about.

I cleaned out two truck fronts when the two Bedfords came back. (N.B.: Medical equipment should be in boxes which *don't* spring open on impact! The Bumble stuff was all over the place and I had to go and get ours from the Halley when the accident happened.) All the men appear to be either in bed snoozing or occupying the shower. Alan is sleeping on *my* bed and snoring as usual. There's a problem about sleeping. I can only find five beds and there ought to be six. If Peter sleeps in the Halley tonight, there is no bed for Alan and me. I will have to ask, I suppose.

It's a real drag to be here for three days. It makes it harder to go on into the danger which is ahead. Not that we've really been idle, but activity has been less than usual, and with solely male company I feel a bit of a lack. I've washed my hair and showered for the second time. Don't know about meals, will just have to wait and see what transpires. Clothing is a problem. Everything is filthy already.

After my shower, went to sit by the sea and read. Denis arrived and we had a chat about this and that, then tea on the terrace. We decided it was a night for a few drinks, so set off for a nearby hostelry.'

The party were joined later by a young mechanic called Liam, who worked for Scottish European Aid (SEA), a relief group engaged in quite significant engineering activities in Bosnia, such as trying to create a new sanitation system in Tuzla. SEA has an office in Split, which it uses as a headquarters. The EDA group was able to use SEA's communications facilities to report the crashes. Liam promised them the use of an SEA Land Rover to avoid driving the trucks into the city the next day.

After a pleasant and relaxing evening, Liam offered to drive some of the party back to the Pension. While reversing his Land Rover, he collided with a parked car which had been invisible in the darkness. Unwisely, he decided to drive away without looking for the car's owner, but the accident had been observed by some Croatian soldiers sitting on the balcony of the hotel. The owner and one of the soldiers followed the Land Rover to the Pension and a tense scene ensued, which ended up with Liam being taken back to the hotel. Paul and Brian went too for security. The owner of the car wanted Liam to pay for the damage, and the two began to negotiate the amount, the owner demanding an exorbitant amount for what was fairly minor damage, and Liam offering instead a very small payment. After a while, one of the soldiers drew and cocked his pistol, at which point Liam admitted defeat and paid the owner £200 in Deutsche Marks. As soon as the money changed hands, the atmosphere was again quite friendly, and the Croats even drove Brian, Paul and Liam back to the Pension.

Meanwhile, Alan and Christine had remained at the Pension, and wanted to go to bed.

'Alan and I had no key and went round the back to see if we could get in, unfortunately rousing Monica, Liam's boss. Like a fool, I spilled the beans. She was far from amused and it was clear Liam was now in deep trouble. He had to pay a lot to buy off the Croatians, and was very unhappy when he found out that Monica knew. I felt terrible. I also felt we'd screwed up the chance of getting the use of the Land Rover for the next day. Telling myself that I'd meant well didn't help. I didn't know that there was a bad relationship between Monica and Liam, because she felt he exceeded the terms of his job. Had I known, I would have tried to keep quiet. Brian and Dave made me feel much happier by being reassuring – perhaps more than I deserved, I don't know. I just hope the poor lad hasn't lost his job as well as his £200. Anyway, we had a whip round to try at least to lessen the pain of the financial loss and gave him £20. I really hate when my basic honesty (or is it stupidity?), gets others into trouble. I wish, in my old age, I could learn sense and discretion.

Plans for the next day were obviously going to be changed. I wanted to wake early enough to catch them before leaving for the garage with the two damaged trucks. Alan and I, after much negotiation, were sleeping in the lads' room. They were in the trucks and Pete and Stewart in the room Denis shared with Claud. Denis and Claud chose to sleep on the balcony and said it was a lovely pleasant night.'

Friday, 25th June 1993. Christine and Alan were able to find a bed for the night, but had to rise at 5.15 am the next morning. Reluctantly, Denis had decided to use their sole surviving truck, the 17 ton Halley moving van for local trips, instead of depending on the SEA Land Rover. Alan recollects: 'I drove the Halley into Split with about eight of us all in the cab. I was the only one with a seat. We drove all around the places with everybody packed

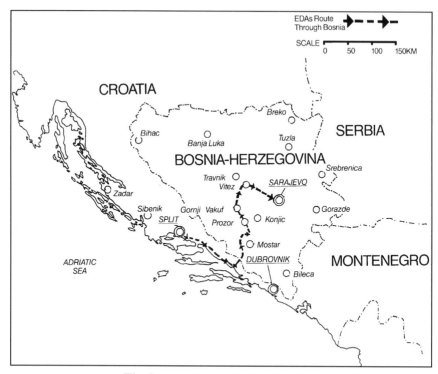

The June route from Split to Sarajevo

in. At checkpoints we would pass out an endless stream of passports, until the policeman would come over and peer into the cab, wondering just how many people were inside.'

After dropping off the two damaged trucks at a garage in Split, they drove out to Trogir to get Brian and Dave's stitches checked at the hospital. The next stop was the refugee camp at Resnik, to deliver medical goods to a Ghanaian doctor married to a Bosnian woman.

'Things are no better there than in March and Josko Tadin was telling us, with real sadness, about the people he had to turn away as the camp is full. The "Ghanaian" doctor is not allowed to practice there because he is Bosnian. He is a surgeon and is wasted merely working in a pharmacy. This sad war is wasting so many lives. Supporting 1,300 refugee families is a huge task. Mr Tadin said that to give each person bread and cheese for breakfast costs 2,000 DM (£800) every day!

From Resnik we went to the Britbat base to see about Brian's UN press pass. We were greeted with the usual courtesy, given coffee and packed lunches, and in due course left satisfied for Split and the garage again. The trucks were progressing well. We waited for a while, in killing heat, then finally went back to Tamarisk, leaving Denis and Claud to wait till the vehicles were ready and bring them back. First stop on returning was a swim and a sun bathe, then a shower and another meal at Pizza Mario. Once again the great quality of this group made it a most enjoyable social occasion. Sometimes the "masculine" nature of the jokes is a bit offputting for an old feminist, but some were so hilarious even an old prude like me had to laugh!!! Tried to phone the kids, but both were out. Bed around midnight, sharing with Alan and Dave. Lovely night's sleep.'

With the trucks repaired, the group could now prepare to move on into Bosnia. Christine had time to note in her diary:

Saturday, 26th June 1993. 'Early rise – what's new? 5.30 am to do my washing so it would be dry for leaving. Had breakfast and went with Claud and Denis and Stewart into Split to a meeting and to pick up some stuff. Then to the NGO meeting which seemed to suggest that there might not be too many problems on our route, though there are many very volatile places still – Mostar, Travnik, Zenica and the Maglaj "finger" are no-go areas still.

Back at Tamarisk, we organized and packed. I'm fed up as I can't find my Reebok trainers. Alan swears he took them into the house, but I've been unable to locate them. Some of the others had been to the market to buy £200 worth of fruit and vegetables which was then loaded into the other vehicles. The usual shambles occurred before leaving time. I was driving the TL, Stewart the Halley and Brian the Bumble. After an initial panic time, my gear changing improved, Dave and Alan being much easier company and less critical. Third to second is still tricky on hills, but the rest are easy – most of the time.

We have now been waiting for two hours (it is now 9.15 pm) at the Bosnia-Hercegovina border with Croatia, waiting for someone to come back with a photocopied pass, then hopefully we'll be on to our destination. This is the longest wait so far. It seems a bit excessive but at least people are nice and friendly and it's a beautiful night for a sit in the sun. When the pass came, which it did eventually, we set off, Dave driving the Bedford TL. Got about 2 km down the road and stopped at a petrol station for Dave and Claud to phone the man at Široki Brijeg [Nevenko Herceg, an official of the Herceg-Bosna Refugee/DP Ministry]. Word came back that he was out, but his wife said she would find him. We settled for another boring wait. After about twenty minutes, we got the word to roll.

Another 80 km of beautiful rural countryside, pretty prosperous looking – villages with well-kept attractive houses – and as darkness fell we reached our destination. Claud asked directions and in the centre of the village we took a left turn – wrongly as it happened – and found ourselves toiling up a long very steep hill. Realizing the mistake, we had to turn – in our case, in very awkward circumstances – and backtrack down the hill again. The Halley had stopped at the bottom and Claud was walking up to meet us. The whole thing then descended into total farce, trucks reversing and manoeuvring, people screaming, strangulated questions down the CB and some priceless gems like Stewart's "Have you got Claud?" which sounds totally unfunny out of context but reduced us in the Bedford to tearful hysterics!

Claud and Denis decided to go to the police to ask for directions and we were instructed to go to a nearby restaurant and have a meal. The trucks were parked with difficulty, and we sallied into what looked a fairly unpromising eating place. They gave us a table outside – why? – and a pooling of everyone's experiences of the day had us all killing ourselves laughing all over again. A round of beers started us off, then we asked for the menu. It came on a plate. A raw pork chop, a sausage and a little cevapcici sausage. The meal, when it arrived was superb. Loads of meat on a big platter, chips, side salad of cucumber, tomato and onion in oil dressing and mustard, plus the usual huge plate of bread.

We had just lifted our forks when the power failed. It was suggested by the pretty dark-haired waitress that we move inside the restaurant as they had an emergency generator. Inside, surrounded by curious locals, we continued our meal which became more and more hilarious. Then Denis and Claud arrived with the news that we had a place to park overnight at a warehouse yard not far away. Denis and Claud had something to eat and asked for the bill. It was 60 marks – 7 marks each (about £2 – £3) for all that food and beer. Marvellous. Collecting the money caused more merriment but eventually we paid, leaving a 10 DM tip for the pretty waitress who had put up with us so pleasantly, even to explaining the distinction between pivo, pira and pivi!!

Back into the vehicles, we headed in pitch dark out of town. Needless to say, we missed our building and went too far, squeezing our way between parked cars at a disco (a lively affair) and then had to turn and come back through! We eventually found the yard, parked and settled for the night, Alan in the TL, Denis in the Bumble and myself in the Halley – on the *bed* for once – lovely. As we settled down, the familiar sounds of gunfire cut through the night, but we reckoned it was just the locals celebrating at their disco.' [There was a wedding in progress, in fact.]

Sunday, 27th June 1993. The morning brought the news that the party would have to stay another day in Široki Brijeg. Christine began to despair.

'We had planned to be ready to go by 8.00 am but, as usual, found that we were going nowhere fast. The problem is that our Sarajevo pass is only good to Vitez. Nothing can be done today, and we must wait till tomorrow. Will we *ever* get home again?

The factory gateman organised for us to use the toilet facilities and got coffee for us. How kind people are to us in situations like these. At this point I'm sitting in the sun on a wall, some of the lads have gone in to play cards, Denis and Claud are negotiating somewhere, I think Brian is listening to music and Alan is going to open up the back so I can get my shorts. What a hard life!

5.45 pm – well, time has passed but it is all a bit frustrating. We're stuck here killing time and it's beginning to look exceedingly unlikely that we'll even get the appropriate pass. My personal opinion is that Nevenko [the official who was supposed to provide them with very good credentials to get through all the checkpoints] does not want to be bothered or that he has been hassled by someone senior and is afraid to do it again – or perhaps that the political situation having changed, he is just less sympathetic. Things improved once Alan rigged up a shower and Claud begged the use of a basin. Everyone washed their "smalls" and generally pottered around. An ice cream lorry came in and we started to negotiate nappies for a box of ice cream. This worked and the ice cream was much enjoyed by everyone around.

The suggestion was then made that some clothes or nappies could be taken to the monastery in the village where a group of refugees from Kaijic had come in only the previous day. Three boxes of nappies and baby clothing were loaded, along with Claud and myself, into a yellow Fiat 500 driven by one of the gate guards. The building the refugees were in was as depressing as these places usually are. It looked as though it had once been a school. Mattresses were laid on the floor covered with grey or brown blankets, no chairs to sit on, children wandering aimlessly, a few men, some old women, one of whom attached herself to us, following us from room to room and smiling. She'd been there a year along with others in her family. I noticed a number tattooed on her arm which suggested she had also been a concentration camp victim.

It's the first time I've actually had to distribute the aid packages myself. People were well behaved (if that's the term I want) and thanked me for what was given. I took as many photographs as I could but always asked first. Without Claud, the language problem would have been insuperable. The women were selective and each was happy with only a few cloth nappies and a few garments. The place was depressing but the facilities were adequate. They had at least shelter, adequate sanitation and food which is provided for them.

Our guide then took us to the church to meet the priest with whom we had a few words before going back to the yard to wait yet again. When we got there, I had a nice surprise. We had put the trucks facing the gate and I was walking towards them, when the two gatemen called me over and presented me with a bunch of roses!!!

A walk to the bar filled an hour or so in the afternoon and then the TL was reorganised yet again. A bit more hanging about chatting, then back to the bar for a great meal and some laughter and talking. I slept out for the first time and enjoyed it till it started to rain in the early hours and I crawled under the truck till morning. The "younger" element stayed out a lot later, talking to (or chatting up) the pretty waitress and some of the young men who were there. Two rounds of drinks were bought *for* us by locals so I guess we can't be too unpopular.'

Brian had an interesting conversation with a very large Croat in the bar. In German, he asked Brian whether he supported Celtic or Glasgow Rangers. In Glasgow, of course, this question is a code for 'Are you Catholic or Protestant?'. Brian evaded the issue by saying they were from Edinburgh, and pointing out the 'Hibs' shirt Stewart was wearing. Croats are staunch Catholics, so it seems certain that this question was asked for exactly the same reason as it would be in Glasgow.

Another sensitive issue which concerned the locals, and police and soldiers at many checkpoints, was the identity of the intended recipients of the relief supplies in the trucks. The best way to deal with this was to simply say that the aid was to be delivered to the hospital in Sarajevo, which treats the injured of all the warring factions.

Monday morning brought heavy rain. Concern about the missing passes was predominant in everyone's thoughts. The plan had been to join an army-escorted convoy to Vitez that day, and it was now doubtful if they could get to the assembly point in time.

'We had breakfast in the canteen and are now waiting for the noted Nevenko to put in an appearance. He was due here at 8.00 am, but it's now 8.40 and there is still no sign of him. It's a bit dreary all this hanging about, and the questions hang heavy about what exactly we will be able to do with the goods we carry if we can't get through. Wonders – Nevenko came up with the passes and within ten minutes we were heading out the gate and up the road towards Tomislavgrad.

Wonderful mountain scenery, a few checkpoints, but the passes worked very well. We made Tomislavgrad just shortly after the time the convoy was due, amazingly. It passed us as we reached the turning into the army camp. Denis nipped in to check if this was *our* convoy and Claud made some photo copies of the all-important pass at the same time. Then it was off after the convoy of fuel trucks.

Unfortunately, a badly placed Prozor sign led us astray into another reversing session but eventually we found ourselves on the dirt road to Prozor – the notorious "Triangle". A checkpoint at the bottom was reasonably quickly negotiated with the help of the UN command truck, but sadly the next bend – a one in four effort of about 25 degree angle on rutted mud, proved too much for the Halley. Alan, unable to get the crawler gear

UN truck prepares to tow the Halley to Camp Redoubt, after its clutch failed on the dirt road road to Prozor

to go in, let Peter try, then Stewart. Their combined efforts, later on, resulted in a burned out clutch.

We had gone on up the road to find a place to pull in. It appeared that a tow was the only way to get the Halley up the hill. We had the tow rope. Denis walked down with it and we waited, escortless. Eventually the lead Land Rover of our escort came back, we explained our difficulty and they stayed with us for a time. Chillingly at one point, both soldiers got their guns and started searching the woods nearby. At last we got a call through to say that they were rolling and would be with us in ten minutes. By this time our convoy was miles ahead but we began to make reasonable progress and, by and large, the road was not as bad as we had feared. The sappers have been doing wonderful work on it, constantly repairing and improving the surface and the drainage. Unfortunately it was not enough for us. The Halley was in front at a section where there was a convoy bypass. After this there was a very steep hill – one in six maybe – clouds of smoke issued from the clutch and after a couple of tries, Peter reversed back down into the bypass and stopped.

We were then faced with a huge dilemma. We had lost our escort, we could not repair a burnt out clutch and the MK would not pull it without the four wheel drive. On top of this, the tow bar was stowed in the back and opening the tailgate would have caused everything to fall down. Initially we tried lightening the vehicle, but this was useless. We then hunted out the tow bar and fittings and tried to assemble them as Brian and Dave tackled the fitting of the four wheel drive. In true female fashion, I put the kettle on and made sandwiches. A picnic 5000 ft up in the Bosnian mountains!

Claud also was practical. He hitch-hiked to the next army camp – a British sapper camp called "Redoubt", indescribably remote and circled with magnificent crags and forests. Here thirty four men work on keeping the road, the only link now into Central Bosnia, open to all traffic, humanitarian and military. Unfortunately, this also includes the HVO [the Croatian armed forces fighting the Muslims in Bosnia.] The captain here was most helpful, organised a tow for the Halley and offered us camp hospitality for the night. A mechanic looked at the Renault and concluded it had to have a new clutch. By this time we had cooked up at the back of the vehicles, as we were too many to feed at the camp. (Boots Instant Meals are *very* tasty.)

Decisions of a painful nature were clearly going to have to be made. The Renault was to be towed to Tomislavgrad and attempts made to find a new clutch in Split. Clearly three people would have to go with it, but which three? I felt in some ways I should volunteer, as potentially the least effective member of the group. But as it was to be my last trip, I wanted to go all the whole way we had planned. Alan felt the same. So we left Denis to make the decision. This was that Peter, Stewart and Dave all go back to Tomislavgrad and then hitch a ride to Split to find whether they could obtain a replacement, bring it up and get the army to fit it. The rest of us were to go on as planned. Really we didn't want to lose any of the group. Each in his own way had played a full part in the success of the group, Stewart and Peter by being keen, chatty, hard working – particularly Stewart – and Dave for similar characteristics plus warmth, humour and unflappability. However, go they did, and hopefully we'll meet up with them again in Split and travel home together as we came down.

Tuesday, 29th June 1993. Reveille was at 5.30 am – nights are so short in Bosnia – and breakfast at quarter past six – usually army food and lots of it. We had decided to head for Gornji Vakuf ourselves and pick up a convoy on the way. What a lovely area this is. The road winds between lines of trees and occasionally opens out to wider views of distant peaks and stony high plains. Then it begins to descend through rural villages, each house with its vegetable plot, its hay stack, its few animals – a peaceful scene – a million miles removed from the war.

It was St Peter's Day and clearly a local holiday, and all the people were either going to or coming from the church. The women all wore dresses with a kind of black pinafore over them and headscarves, also black. They seemed quite friendly and responded to my wave with smiles and waves. On the road to Prozor is the most beautiful lake surrounded by wooded hills and pretty clusters of red-tiled houses. A narrow neck of land with an island shaped hill projects into its incredibly turquoise-blue waters – in the distance are high jagged peaks all silhouetted against the vivid blue of a hot June sky.

Leaving this beauty we dropped down into Prozor – a busy town, recently very violent with many burned out ruined buildings in the centre. People milled about and there were many men in uniform, mean looking men with hand grenades in their pockets and muddy boots. [The Croats had just lost a major battle, and were pulling back into Prozor.] They kept asking us where we were taking the aid, and accusing us of helping the Muslims. We *had* to take on fuel and went to the town's only garage, where the response was none too friendly. We began to get a very uncomfortable gut feeling about the place and were extremely happy to leave it and begin the long steep climbs to the summit of the Gornji Vakuf road. Half way up there was a most welcome UN tank containing British soldiers. We stopped to inquire about the situation, and were told it was safe to proceed as Gornji Vakuf had been quiet for the past few days. The road is frequently used by UNHCR convoys, but unfortunately they go far too fast for us. We have no chance of staying with them.

The views down over Prozor are amazing, and we stayed long enough to chat to the soldiers and have some coffee, bread and cheese, and what not (what not being defined in my personal dictionary as trips to the loo!). After that, I drove for a while, fairly adequately, though a few gear changes had Denis tutting. Gornji Vakuf was lined with children waving, and in some cases pointing to their mouths. This war is going to create a generation of children with rotten teeth. I don't like the begging aspect, never now give sweets.

At the base we quickly met up with a rather young (26) and pretty lady doctor [Captain Marion Cjakowska, known as "CJ", Regimental Medical Officer with the Prince of Wales Own Regiment], who is now helping out the "Hearts and Minds" project in this area. She is quite tall, and carries a large gun at her hip. She says "I'm a non-combatant, so I only get a pistol." Her prime job is to look after the mental and physical well-being of the soldiers here, but the UN brief allows her to also involve herself in the aid effort. The soldiers here regularly ferry supplies to remote villages and try to become involved in other projects like repairing the Muslim Health Centre in the village.

From at least one soldier, we got strongly the opinion that the Muslims are in *all* ways less extreme. If they take prisoners, they only take men, while the other side takes old folk, women and kids as well. They do *not* torch houses and they have not been known to destroy churches. This is one man's point of view, and others may feel differently. Steve [Tumbler, an officer at Redoubt] echoed the words I've heard from many out here, "There are no good sides in this war. On each side are good men and bad men." It seems to me that the good must face a moral dilemma, not knowing how to square their conscience and the way their government and peer pressure makes them act.

We unloaded the goods we had brought from Hull and had cups of tea and chats. The Bumble was causing difficulty with steering problems since our accident and was *very* difficult to drive and slow on hills, annoying Denis, who thought it could go faster. The garage in Split had repaired it without having all the necessary parts, and some of the bolts which were supposed to hold the steering gear together were just pushed into the holes, with no thread left to keep them secure! The army mechanic said we were lucky the wheel hadn't come off. It was in a pretty dangerous condition. He did a temporary repair which took nearly two hours. It was obvious even before we spoke to a Captain Mick Hines that it was unlikely we'd be going on today. His information was that a Sheffield group had been shot at the other day, even with a UN convoy or escort, and that patrols were withdrawn from the roads at 6.00 pm and no one was advised to be out after that.

The decision was made that we were staying, so another afternoon of sitting in the sun killing time followed the quick unpacking of all the Gornji Vakuf boxes. It was clear they would appreciate more things if they were available. Looks like they'll get the whole Renault load. It is going to be a long time fixing, as the part has to be sent out from Britain by air. Goodness knows when that will be there.

We occupied ourselves with a bit of washing and a bit of writing and a bit of jogging, a bit of shoe cleaning (Claud) and a bit of snoozing – eventually Denis! (Jogging was a little risky, as snipers were active in the area. One section of the camp perimeter was particularly hazardous, and joggers, which included Brian and Denis, were advised to pass that section at a gallop!) Tea was 5 – 6 pm but rescheduled to 7.30 and finally to 8.30. It wasn't that marvellous when it came, but it filled a space and the special taste of rakija before was exceedingly nice. By this time we knew that the Bumble was at least safer to drive if not easier and that we had an escort to get up to Vitez the next day.

We also had a space in a shed to sleep but only Claud and Denis used it. Alan kipped in the Bedford and Paul and Brian in the space under the Bumble. I started in the shed but decided a move to the TL would be quieter and slept underneath. It's amazingly pleasant sleeping out like that, though I missed my pillow and was also a little chilly by 5.00 am.

Wednesday, 30th June 1993. Rose around 6.00 am and went for a shower, but ended up just with a wash. Had breakfast and tidied up and, arrayed in flak jackets and helmets, awaited our convoy at the front gate. They arrived fifty minutes late at 9.40 am. The Gornji Vakuf to Vitez road is picketed at significant points by UN patrols – about six in all, I think. The UN vehicles went first followed by the TL and then the Bumble.

We hoped we were going to be able to keep up. Just before we left, Denis had come and said he had been in touch with Jeanne, and Julie had left the message that everything was fine. I surprised myself by getting quite teary about this. I was travelling in the Bumble with Paul and Brian. Alan was driving the TL with Claud and Denis, who was helping him, of course, with his gear changes!

The road seemed better than the last time we were over it, but was, of course, very dusty and the potholes were still a reason for careful manouevring. We passed the fish farm where the Italians [aid workers] were killed. Apparently they had run away. Two had escaped, two had been shot running and one was shot and then bayoneted. Not pleasant. However, our journey was without mishap and people even seemed quite friendly. There is so much evidence of normal life going on that it's hard to imagine that this area has been subject to a terrible and bloody conflict.

Captain Mark Bower met us on our entry to the Vitez camp and spent quite a while briefing us on the situation. He told a quite different tale from the Gornji Vakuf officer, Mick Hines. Apparently there has been a big Muslim push from the north and the south and the Croats have been squeezed into an ellipse-shaped area starting at Vitez. The Muslims want this, and are systematically clearing all areas of Croat families. This has been caused by the successor to the Vance Owen plan. Under the new plan, the Serbs would be able to keep what they'd gained. The Muslims therefore want to secure as much territory as they can prior to this. They want *all* Croats out of the area and have been killing animals and desecrating churches just like the Croats did to them in other areas. However, it does seem we may be able to move fairly freely, at least to Zenica and even, possibly, to Kiseljak.

First priority on arriving was to eat, and the food here is terrific – marvellous choice and loads of it – then to see to repairs to the Bumble. It transpired that the Gornji repairs had not held and that the vehicle was again in a potentially lethal state. Something radical had to be done and it was, by the REME work shop at Vitez, but there are no guarantees that we'll be able to get it back to Edinburgh, though we will obviously try.

Denis's attempts to contact people by phone and fax were fruitless and it was finally decided that we should hitch a ride with UNPROFOR to Travnik to see if he could find Mr Duić. Denis hoped to borrow his car to drive to Kiseljak, in order to negotiate our entry to Sarajevo with the Serbs there. Mr Duić could not be found, but Denis was told that he was still alive and living in the town.

We had our meal, spent some pleasant time at the Dutch Communications Centre, and finally retired in our desirable residence, open to the stars at the sides and slept, despite a large mortar which landed near the officers mess during the night and the intermittent shooting – machine guns, mortars and single shots which passed over our heads from the Croats on one side to the Muslims on the other side of valley. Apparently our tent was directly in between them. We hoped no one was a bad aimer!

(NB. Forgot to mention that during the afternoon, Gen. Philippe Morillon came to Vitez to make his farewell speech to the British troops there. We had a grandstand view and Brian got a chance to ask a question about his attitude to the aid agencies and the job that they were doing.)

Thursday, 1st July 1993. It looked like it was going to be a boring day with very little to do, but in the end it was very interesting, not to say exciting. After breakfast Denis, Paul and Claud went off to Travnik again and succeeded in locating Mr Duić, a Croat who had previously worked for the IRC and who had befriended some EDA people in 1992. They found Duić in a state of severe depression – his late father's house in a Croat village outside Travnik had been partly razed, the village inhabitants expelled, everything looted, including his car and all his family possessions. So far, he had not been molested personally. Denis promised to do what he could to get him employment as an interpreter, or to try to help him get out of the country. (He has a UN blue card due to his IRC employment. But his wife has no card.) Such is the fate of a Croat in a Muslim town.

Since attempts to borrow a car to go to the Kiseljak had failed, it was obviously going to be necessary to use the Bedford TL, which meant it had to be unloaded into the tent next to ours.

Brian had arranged to go out with Capt. Mark Bower and his team to a number of places in the vicinity and I managed to talk my way into going too. Poor Alan drew the short straw and got left in the base. We went off in two Land Rovers with Mark, Brian and Dobrilla (Debi) the interpreter in one, and myself with Scott McHugh and Philip Moffitt in the other, both of them Lance Corporals.

Our first stop was ICRC in Zenica, then on to the village of Preočica to enquire about the location of a doctor. The road climbed high behind Zenica through beautiful scenery. We had one check point to negotiate through – helped by Debi – and then it was on to a twisty windy road passing between the houses of the village and squeezing past cars and people. Lots of kids came out, hoping, I suppose, for sweets. They were the poorest we had seen. Apparently this village has had no aid at all. I asked if I could photograph them and was not allowed to do so. Brian, Debi and Mark went into the "hospital" to find out about the doctor, but she was not there. They succeeded in locating her the next day and taking her to Stari Vitez where her services were needed.

This village (Preočica) is high on the hills immediately behind Vitez and has a fantastic view over the valley below. We came back down into Zenica, went briefly to UNHCR, then headed back to Vitez. We had our coffee out of *real* cups with saucers in the Officers' Mess. Our drivers were interested to know what it was like inside, as they never get to see it. We had a brief glimpse of Samantha Fox, in orange cutaway shorts, there on a publicity visit, presumably intended to cheer up the troops. Most we spoke to were singularly unimpressed but they went along with the "fun" of the occasion all the same.

A report had been received by the UN of a possible atrocity, the murder of three children in a remote village in the hills above Gornji Vakuf. Our next job was to investigate this. Debi, the interpreter, was really upset by this. She's obviously an intelligent and sensitive girl, a former teacher of English, who feels deeply what her people are doing to each other. She had been particularly distressed by Ahimici, and the mortar going off so close the previous night at 5:30 am had brought back all the feelings as it was the same time that Ahimici was attacked.

We drove to the T-junction at Novi Travnik past the two gutted buses from the "Convoy of Joy" [a refugee convoy which was caught in crossfire at the intersection] and up into the hills from a UN picket at the summit of the road. This is the farthest I have ever been from the main routes. Our

Off on patrol–Christine and 'Debi' (Dobrilla) Kalaba, an interpreter at the British base in Vitez. Debi was killed by a sniper the same day as Christine

road was little more than a rutted track climbing higher and higher through woodland until it opened out onto the high slopes. Real bandit country. The first village we came to, Mirkoviči, had not one intact house remaining. The lead Land Rover pulled up at a group of people – men and children – and, with a slightly sick sense of anticipation, we waited to hear if this was the place. Philip and Scott were hoping that it wasn't to be a case of searching the houses as they thought they might be booby trapped. *We* also had to face the fact that any bodies would have to be transported in our Land Rovers and, as the lads pointed out, the civilian body bags are clear, not like the black ones used for soldiers. This, however, was not the place so we went on.

The track degenerated into something which would be considered pretty rough as a mountain track in Glencoe! At places we were tilted to an alarming sideways angle and sometimes actually proceeding down the river bed. The story was the same at the next two villages. People smiled and were friendly and helpful. There was no sense of concealment and no feeling on our part of fear. Either, it seemed, the story was fabricated, or we had not found the correct village. It seemed, as Debi said, surprising that it should only be children. If there had been an atrocity of an ethnic nature, one would also expect adult bodies.

We came back down to the road and headed for Novi Travnik. As we approached the next village, it occurred to me to ask what protection the sides of the Land Rover would give against bullets. I was told "none"! Seconds later there was an outburst of firing – very, very close. The lead Land Rovers speeded up and we followed. I was later told there had been five bursts of firing and that nearly thirty rounds had been fired. They seemed to be firing at us, though we were later told that opposing sides had been firing across the valley and we were simply in the way. Be that as it may, it didn't alter the immediate sensation of being under fire for the first time. The primary feeling was not fear at all, but an adrenaline rush of exhilaration. As we approached Novi Travnik, the presence of people on the road and in the gardens indicated that the immediate danger was over.

Our next port of call was to be Stari Vitez. This satellite town of Vitez itself is a tiny Muslim enclave encircled by HVO. We were going to what was called the hospital, but which was simply one room with two stretcher type beds and a few shelves of drugs and medicines. We met the lady doctor and two nurses, had coffee and a chat. Anyone injured in the frequent shelling or random sniping has first treatment there. We heard of a child who had been shot in the head. Someone crept through HVO lines in the dark to get help from the UN camp, who then came in and transported the child to hospital in Zenica, where, thankfully, she is recovering. The centre of Stari Vitez is a scene of Berlin style devastations. The worst that I've seen so far. There's a huge hole where a mortar landed, and a wrecked and rusting vehicle sits in the middle of it; the buildings around are wrecked shells. The dispensary is an island of sanity where ordinary human converse is continued, and yet they have so much to cope with, in the way of the dreadful things they see and the problems they have to handle. Even the welcome visits of UN personnel sometimes bring more problems to them, in that they can trigger violence. However, they said they wanted the UN to keep on coming.

We left there, thinking our day was done but we still had to take Debi to her parents' home in Novi Travnik. At the dispensary, the UN folk had been given a gift of eggs because they had tried to bring some up from Split for egg sandwiches and they'd got broken – not surprisingly! At first there were five eggs, but people came to the door with several others until there were nine. Debi was taking them to her folks. We waited in the car, pestered by children wanting sweets, who then kicked the Land Rover when they were not obliged. Things got so nasty, the escort got out and walked menacingly round the cars.

When Debi came out, we went off towards the T-junction again. A Warrior (APC) with soldiers, sitting at the junction, waved in an unusual way. It was noted and we immediately turned and drove into the waste ground parking area. It transpired there was a major battle going on, centred on controlling the junction, and we were right in the middle of it. We got out of the Land Rover and stood at the one side. Capt. Bower said that we should get into the ditch if the shooting came too close, and then headed for the Warrior. With simple minded self sacrifice, Brian and I both went to get our helmets out of the Land Rovers so we wouldn't lose them!! We stood listening to the shells (and having a ballistics lesson on what were incoming and what outgoing).

Suddenly, there was one with a totally different sound. It had passed 5 m above our heads, and was either a badly aimed shot for us or a warning shot to get the hell out of the area. The Captain did just that. We were ordered curtly into the Land Rover which shot off at top speed towards Vitez. A mile or so down the road again, there were people around, so we knew the immediate danger was over.'

****

Christine's diary ends at this point. During the three days of life which remained to her, too many things were happening, and she had no time to write up her diary. The story of these dramatic days will be told mainly in Brian's words, as spoken into a tape recorder, with additional details drawn from Denis's diary.

****

Friday, 2nd July 1993. 'After reloading the TL, we set out to drive to Kiseljak via Zenica. Our original intent had been to drive right through to Sarajevo, but checkpoint delays made that impossible. We were soon in trouble at an HVO checkpoint on the Vitez-Zenica road. The Croatian militiamen wanted the trucks driven to their police station in Buskovaća, where they are currently holding three members of a French NGO team. Claud managed to talk them into his going along in a police car, so that they could examine and copy the permit provided by Nevenko Herceg back in Široki Brijeg. We were rescued by the arrival of two Warriors, commanded by Dominic Hastings, a supremely confident, black, British sergeant. With his support, the convoy was eventually allowed to proceed.

We reached Kiseljak, the jumping off point to the front lines, at 2.00 pm. The Herceg-Bosna pass was again questioned at the HVO checkpoint on the Visoko road. In February, EDA had tried to get through to Sarajevo, but had had to abandon this attempt at Kiseljak because of difficulties with the same Croatian militia. One man there remembered us from February, and asked to see our documentation for the Serbs – "no problem, but we would like to see it". After successfully evading this threatening question, Denis dumped the incriminating documents in a rubbish container at the first opportunity.

We were told that we would have to go to the HVO headquarters for a permit to proceed further. Claud went inside to bandy words with five aggressive men, who all crowded into a tiny room with him, but stopped short of physical violence. Eventually, one of them signed the confirmatory order. It was now too late to go on into Sarajevo. We knew that the next stage of the journey was going to involve hours and hours of checkpoint holdups.

This was the place where Alan's shoes became hostages for a radio telephone. Denis went to see John Fox at the UNHCR office, and managed to borrow the radio to contact the UN base at Sarajevo airport. Alan remarked to Denis "He was very trusting, giving you that walky-talky." Denis, with a very crestfallen look, admitted that he had had to leave Alan's shoes and his two cameras as a deposit!

We camped overnight at a warehouse on the outskirts of the town. The paved parking area was adjacent to a newly mown hayfield, making a very pleasant setting for a picnic meal of "compo" rations "liberated" from the base at Vitez – goulash and rice and tinned apple pie. After eating, we laid out the sleeping bags under the starry sky, and enjoyed a quiet night's sleep.
Saturday, 3rd July 1993. This was a very poignant and frustrating morning. Another Sarajevo-bound convoy had also parked at the yard the previous night. Our plan had been to let them leave a little ahead of us, and then catch up with them at the first checkpoint. They duly went storming off down the road, only to reappear shortly afterwards. This was the weekend in early July when access to Sarajevo became even more difficult than before. The Serbs had seized supplies from an aid convoy, and the UN had responded by refusing to deliver any further aid to them. Effectively, there were no UNHCR convoys running into Sarajevo.

We sat round and talked it through. The decision was that that day we were going to move, we weren't going to stay in Kiseljac, and that when we moved, we were either going on to Sarajevo or back to Vitez, and if we went back to Vitez, that was it – we would keep on heading for home, and Sarajevo was scrubbed. Everyone was sitting around the yard wondering what was going to happen, when Denis and Claud, who had gone to see John Fox again, came rolling back into the yard and said "Right, that's it, we're going". It all seemed a bit of an anticlimax. We had been preparing for what seemed like weeks to go to Sarajevo, and it all seemed too casual or too offhand for somebody just to walk in and say "Start the truck up, we're going to Sarajevo", just like that!

Denis and Claud had been able to obtain clearance as far as Sarajevo airport, but not all the way into the city. It was too dangerous for anything except armoured vehicles that morning. We left, and got as far as the HVO checkpoint on the outskirts of Kiseljak. The guard looked at the permit that Claud had obtained the previous day at the HVO headquarters, and said "I'm not accepting that – it's a forgery." The TL went back into town, where Denis and Claud (with difficulty) sorted things out. Then all the scowls became "sweetness and light". There was never anything in the middle – it was either a scowl or a smile. And that was us outside the HVO and heading for the strip that's controlled by the Serbs who are encircling Sarajevo. To get there, you have to cross three front lines – first the Croat HVO, then the Serb beseigers and finally the Bosnian government defence perimeter. We were now "one down and two to go".

Soon after you leave the HVO checkpoint, the real problems start, because you've got the first of the Serb militiamen checkpoints. That's where they dismantle the trucks, open all the boxes. Some of the boxes were labelled as educational materials, with donations of children's books to be used in schools. They started rushing off with these books, trying to find somebody who could read them, or who knew what they were. They seemed to have a paranoia about any kind of propaganda going in or out of the city. They were very determined to go through everything in the trucks. People who had been there before said that they had never searched like that before. Everything was getting ripped open, and they were really hostile.

Denis was asked if we had any "technical items". He told them we had a diathermy machine for the hospital and other medical supplies. It's usual for the Serbs to take a third of all aid going into Sarajevo, and Denis was prepared for that. He asked them simply "Please don't damage things, as then they are not fit for anyone." They then sent for a more senior officer, an unpleasant individual, who in turn brought in someone who was supposed to be a doctor from the military hospital. He was probably a pharmacist, and was unshaven and surly. He said that his hospital hadn't seen stuff like this for over a year, and wanted it all. The senior officer then stated that they were going to "temporarily seize the goods, for analysis", and that we could pursue enquiries at Ilija police station. They took everything – thousands of pounds worth of drugs and instruments. That was the worst part. It was just a total frustration to have to sit there and watch it.

With the strange kind of double standard, having stolen all our equipment and supplies, they then proceeded to issue us a receipt. To make matters worse, while all the boxes were still spread all over the ground waiting to be reloaded into the trucks, a tremendous thunderstorm started. The rain was bouncing off the road for about half-an-hour, while we tried desperately to keep things dry in case they got spoiled. Christine was heard to speculate that perhaps a bolt of lightning might blow them away and solve all of our problems!

After a long wait for a militia car to escort us, we were taken down to the so-called "Serbian Red Cross" warehouse, where they would still take one third of what was left. Everything had to be sorted, so they could take a proportion of the items in each category – food, clothes, even the educational materials. They were business-like and reasonably pleasant. They accepted our accounting and didn't push it.

We now had another long wait for an escort. By this time it was 6.30 pm. We called the UNHCR man at the airport on the radio telephone to ask if it was safe to proceed. He told us it was OK as far as the airport, but that the road to the PTT (the Post, Telegraph and Telecommunications building where the UN has its headquarters in Sarajevo, which lies midway between the airport and the centre of the city) was "closed" after 7.00 pm. He also confirmed that we could stay over at the airport. As we approached the airport, we passed through a sector which is very close to where the lines are between the Serbs on the outside of the city and the Bosnians on the inside. The road here is protected somewhat from sniper fire by a massive fence built out of railway sleepers. What would be more or less a double circle of Serb and Bosnian lines is interrupted just by the airport. Everything inside the airport perimeter is under UN control. It just prevents the circle around the city from actually becoming complete circles. It also means that the road leading to the airport is the only way out of Sarajevo. This is the road now known as "Snipers' Alley".

We duly arrived at the airport just on 7.00 pm. The situation now descended into farce. The French UN guard at the gate told us: "It is too dangerous for you to proceed to the PTT, so you must stay here. But we can't let you in without a permit from the UN Civil Police, who are stationed at the PTT." Denis asked for clarification: "We must go from the airport to the PTT to get a pass to allow us to sleep at the airport, so that we can then come back to the airport from the PTT, because it's too dangerous to drive from the airport to the PTT?" Exactly.

With no alternative but to continue into the city, we now had to turn the trucks around in a very unsavoury place, a little narrow alley leading into the airport. It was quite intimidating there, because all round the airport

The road known as Snipers' Alley, near where Christine was shot

they have been around with bulldozers and just made big piles of earth, so you're not too far away from something that's probably about head height to provide shelter from incoming fire. There was also lots of traffic coming in and out, and it adds more of a sense of urgency than we had seen before at any of the other busy sections for UN traffic.

We now headed towards the city along Snipers' Alley, which at one time must have been the main road into the city – a big four-lane motorway which runs all the way from the airport to the UN offices at the old post office building. It takes you past the Holiday Inn, which has effectively become the Press Centre in Sarajevo. There was only one halt on that stretch of the road to check the way. It no longer matters which side of the road you drive on – there's not really enough traffic to worry about it. At one point, we were coming down the motorway driving on the correct side, and for some reason or other, the road was blocked. We had to go across onto the other side of the road, and then continue on.

We were stopped at a new Serb checkpoint between the airport and the UN checkpoint, but in sight of French armoured personnel carrier. The Serbs at first demanded to search the trucks again, but Claud was able to talk them out of it. So we arrived finally at the PTT, and carried straight on into Sarajevo. We passed a mixture of high rise buildings and ordinary housing. A lot of the high rises are damaged – you can see that there are holes through them, or there are sections that have got no windows left. Sometimes you can see where there has been damage that has been repaired. One very prominent building – a really big high rise of twenty stories or so – both sides have partially collapsed, just leaving this finger sticking up in the middle. Even the Holiday Inn has sign of at least one impact.

We couldn't keep our eyes off the scenes of destruction. One of the things that makes it even harder to take is that people still seem to be acting perfectly normally, the way they walk about, with all the tramcars lying higgledy-piggledy along the road, all damaged and shelled, rubbish lying everywhere. Probably the most worrying moment was when we missed our way at one point. We all stopped, and it was very very open, and felt very exposed. Over on the right was a block of housing, and the ground from the housing came down into almost a ditch. It was quite a shallow slope that came up again on the other side, forming a big dip, which was full of people. We were stopped, and they all started shouting at us. We were all looking at each other and thinking: "What do they know that we don't know? We should not be here!" Brian admitted to feeling a "wee bit dry around the mouth" at that point. Christine was heard murmuring a little snatch of an old gospel song – something about "standing in the need of prayer."

At 7.30 pm, we finally arrived at the Kosovo hospital. When we pulled into the hospital grounds, we couldn't believe it really. The last couple of days had seen this target of getting into Sarajevo dangled and then taken away several times, and then suddenly, without any ceremony, without actually meaning to, we were there, at the hospital!

We were met by Prof Smajkić, who directed us into the hospital's underground carpark. We unloaded our supplies straight away to reduce the risk of theft, which is greater when more people are about during the day. Even so, a few items disappeared, but most of them were safely deposited in a locked store. A few medical items had survived, a printer for Prof. Smajkić, almost all the personal parcels, the Sarajevo-Edinburgh boxes, and three to four tons of general food and toiletries.

When the hospital people insisted on feeding us, we swallowed our qualms about consuming any of their very limited supplies, and enjoyed the first food any of us had had for many hours, trying to be polite and not appear too greedy. They insisted that they had plenty food – there had been a birthday party that day for one of the girls who worked at the hospital – the shelling had been so bad that not everybody could make it – it won't keep to tomorrow – you've got to eat it! There was hardly any light in the hospital – they have very little emergency power. We had a plate each, but there were not enough knives and forks to go around.

We slept that night in a room at the hospital. There were no windows, and we were given candles to provide a little light. Denis, rapt in thought as he talked about something, leaned back a little too far and a candle set fire to the back of his shirt. We were just off the main public reception area, and on a Saturday night there was nobody there. Every time you walked about, your footsteps were clattering and echoing and there was hardly any light. It was all rather strange.

There were endless discussions about which of the toilets was the least foul. It really is an abiding memory – absolutely dreadful. There is no water in Sarajevo, so none of the sanitation systems are working, even in the hospital. The waste is piled on the floor, and you have to pick your way through it. Every so often, someone will clear it away, but there is no water to clean up afterwards. This is the kind of thing that never makes headlines. You get all the smoke and flames on the television news, you hear all the statistics about how little food is getting in and what people have got to eat, and then they'll say "Oh, the water's been turned off." The last thing, perhaps, that comes into your mind is that it means that you're also going to spend all night sleeping beside the most stinky, appalling toilet that you've ever come across in your life.

We never had a chance to visit any of the wards – we were actually very pushed for time, and there were lots of things that we could have done, and would have done, had time permitted. Denis actually wanted to stay longer in Sarajevo, but was persuaded against this by the rest of the party, who wanted to deliver their supplies and head for home.

Sunday, 4th July 1993. We had breakfast at the hospital – bread rolls and a cold drink. Claud managed to locate an old friend, Mr Bukvić, a very famous Yugoslav footballer from the fifties and sixties. He was quite overcome by Claud's unexpected appearance on his doorstep. Later, Denis and Claud met the Foreign Minister of Bosnia-Hercegovina, on behalf of Scottish Action for Bosnia.

The rest of us, guided by Maureen Cerkez and her husband Fadil, got a tour of the Turkish quarter and the city centre. Maureen works for UNHCR, and manages to feed several Sarajevo families by eating very little herself and spending most of her salary on food to give to them. She is oblivious to personal danger and travels around Sarajevo without concern for snipers or shellfire. She was more concerned for our safety than her own. Every so often, we had to scuttle up alleys or hide in doorways when the mortars came in. When things were getting too close, for some reason or other, you could feel the air changing. I have no idea what it is, whether it is something that's just coming past, or whether it's because you're starting to get close enough to feel the blast, but without any training or any explanation you just start to feel within yourself that some of the noises, some of the things that happen, are more worrying than others. Without actually knowing why. And certainly some of the sounds are very unnerving. Sometimes you feel as though there's been an explosion or an impact, but after that you've got this consciousness of bits of metal flying about and zinging off things and that's a very different feeling. The thing that I think always got me was that it was all so sudden. There was no long rumbling thunder-like explosion; there are just very quick sharp sounds. And sometimes there's this feeling almost like a hand pressing down on your head. And you wonder what on earth might happen in that split second. It's very fast. You know the way that some people look at spiders – and don't like the way that they zip about because they have that feeling that you can't do anything about it, you can't catch them. It's that same sort of no-warning, no-buildup. You don't get time to prepare yourself, it's just suddenly something's happened. And you don't know when the next one's going to come.

There was one point when Maureen confidently said "Oh, let's just stand out of the way here", (up against the wall, traditional style). And she said "These things usually come in threes." Just as she finished speaking, the fourth one went off. If she'd told us they came in threes, and we'd heard three, we'd have walked off quite happily. But because we'd heard a fourth one, you just didn't know when it was going to stop. And then at one point, there was an impact that was close enough. We were walking along a main street, coming towards a section like a wee park square, just a few trees and flower beds, and as we approached that there was a *bang!* just around the corner and we could see the earth and soil and smoke come flying across the street in front of us. And that must have been maybe 100 metres away. The street was deserted in seconds.

In the afternoon, Maureen arranged a party for everyone at Tomislav Leitner's flat. There was Coke that Maureen had bought at the UN canteen, a couple of bottles of whisky, nuts and crisps. We contributed some "compo" rations, some food which was cooked on the last of his gas, more whisky. We had a very nice afternoon, just talking in wee groups – Mr Bukvić, Arif Smajkić, Maureen, Fadil, Tom and ourselves. Bukvić, the footballer, picked up the guitar out of the corner and started to play these plaintive folk songs. Everyone sang and sometimes cried.

Tom, our host, was a dentist, but also a cosmetic surgeon! His flat was obviously an incredibly desirable piece of property. Tom took us down at one point and showed us where he was born. This had been his family house and he was born there, and so that made it all the more poignant. He had very big windows on two sides of his main room and both of those windows were looking towards the hills outside the city. And you know that when you are looking towards the hills, effectively, you are looking at, (for him anyway) the other side. Beautiful big picture windows they must have been, but now they're all criss-crossed with sticky tape, to try and stop them shattering. And everything, absolutely everything, in that flat is warm and domestic. The paintings are obviously his – they're not bought prints or anything like that, they're all originals. And other bric-a-brac that has obviously been treasured – bits of pottery, plates on the wall.

We stayed there late into the evening. We sat out on the balcony, drank coffee and watched the flares and tracer bullets. (The Serbs shoot parachute flares into the sky to light up the airport runway, and shoot anyone who is trying to escape from Sarajevo by crossing it.) We were probably breaking the law by sitting outside after curfew. The highlight of the evening was when we were invited to sleep there, instead of having to return to the stench of the room at the hospital. We all got beds – they were all clean and all comfortable – these must have been the best things we ever had to sleep on during that whole trip. Apart from the fact that it was a very noisy night with all the shooting, it was wonderful.

Monday, 5 July 1993. In the morning, we had our closest miss during heavy shelling. We were just about to turn into the market, when a mortar bomb landed there and killed fifteen people. If it had come only moments later, we would have already turned the corner, and probably all of us would have been killed.

Later that morning we visited an Institute making artificial limbs and rehabilitating the 700+ war amputees in Sarajevo. [That number includes over 300 children.] Normally they work three shifts round the clock, but since there had been neither power nor running water in the city for the last three weeks, everything had come to a halt – all for the want of thirty litres of fuel a day. We decided that most of the aid we brought in would go to support the Institute's patients and workers.

We went back to the hospital for speeches of thanks and presentations by Prof. Smajkić and the Institute of Public Health. An incredible lunch of home-made traditional spicy and sweet bakes was then served. We asked how it was cooked, and were told that Mrs Smajkić had burned an old chair – probably the last of their fuel, sugar and spices.

At 1.00 pm, we said our last farewells, put our flak jackets on, reversed the trucks out of the underground parking garage, and set out towards the PTT and the airport. We were all feeling pretty upbeat – the trucks were empty, we had done our job, we're going home! We intended to be in Vitez that evening. We made one wrong turning, but soon recovered. We had to stop at the Bosnian government checkpoint before the PTT to confirm our clearance. There was a ten minute delay, as they didn't seem to expect us, but we were soon rolling along again.

A mile beyond the PTT, just before we reached the last Bosnian checkpoint under the overpass at the junction to the airport road, a single shot was fired from somewhere to the south of the road. Alan, Claud and Denis, who were in the lead truck, didn't know that Christine had been hit until we all stopped under the overpass a few seconds later. A Cable News Network (CNN) armoured vehicle appeared on the scene almost instantly. The two CNN reporters brought out a stretcher, Christine was rushed into the CNN car, Alan jumped in the back, and they drove off at breakneck speed with the door still open. Alan braced his legs across the vehicle to stop them from sliding out.

The armoured car arrived a few minutes later at the French military hospital, about a mile away at the PTT. For a few terrible moments, the French guard refused to let them into the compound. Alan shouted at him to open the gates, which he finally did. Stretcher bearers rushed Christine into the hospital building, placed her on a trolley and raced through the corridors with Alan running after them, right into the operating theatre. Alan sat in a corner of the theatre, while the surgeons tried desperately to save Christine's life. The two CNN men, Mike and Brian, sat with their arms round Alan and talked to him. After about half-an-hour, Alan was told that Christine was dead. The heavy calibre bullet had passed right through her, severing the aorta. She never knew what hit her, and certainly felt no pain.'

Dobrilla (Debi), the interpreter working with Mark Bower who had gone out with Christine and Brian four days earlier, was shot dead while walking in the grounds of the Vitez base that same evening.

10

Return
to
Glencoe

Triumph had turned to tragedy with shocking suddenness. The rest of the party were escorted out to the airport, where they left the trucks and were driven back to Sarajevo in UN vehicles. Brian and Denis tried to get a report back to Edinburgh. At this point, they had been told that Christine had serious arm and chest wounds, and had been transferred to Kosovo hospital. Denis's wife, Jeanne, contacted Elspeth with this information. When the sad truth was received two or three hours later, Elspeth's son, Mark, was the first to know, and had to break the news to Alistair, calling from Vancouver. Jeanne travelled to Wishaw to notify and comfort Julie and Paul. Elspeth had the tragic duty of telling her mother, Jessie.

Back in Sarajevo, most of the group spent the night again at Tom's flat. Alan could not face going back to Tom's – the happy memories of the previous night were too poignant to bear – so he and Brian slept at Maureen's. Streams of people came to offer their sympathy – Tom, Arif Smajkić, neighbours.

The UN had promised to get Alan home quickly. Early the next morning, two white Land Rovers picked everyone up and took them back to the airport. Brian was to accompany Alan by air. The rest of the party were to drive the now empty trucks out.

(After a very slow trip, with more trouble from the HVO in Kiseljak and long waits for clearance at many points, they finally made it back to Gornji Vakuf, where they were reunited with the other third of the party. With the generous voluntary help of British army mechanics at Tomislavgrad, and parts flown out by EDA from Edinburgh, they had managed to get the

Halley truck repaired. Its nine ton load was left with Captain Cjakowska and her team, to help the many families and refugees in great need in the areas patrolled by the Prince of Wales Own Regiment. Specialised medical and surgical goods were delivered to Tuzla, Zenica and other hospitals.)

Moments after the Canadian Hercules aircraft landed at the Sarajevo airport, its cargo of relief supplies was pushed out onto the runway. Alan and Brian had to run across the tarmac, jump into the plane and strap in immediately, since the Hercules is too big a target to remain on the ground for more than a few seconds. As soon as they were in, the doors were closed and the Hercules lumbered down the runway, lifted its wheels and climbed steeply out of the danger zone. The Canadian crew members watched intently through the porthole windows until the aircraft was clear of any threat of attack from the ground. Forty-five minutes later, the Hercules landed at Ancona in Italy.

Even at times like this, the bureaucratic system must be satisfied. Flight reservations, arrangements for the return of Christine's body to Scotland, transfer of funds to pay expenses, all had to be dealt with, and quickly. Officials of the British Consulate and the UNHCR at Ancona did everything they could to speed the process and clear any obstacles. A British Airways flight was leaving shortly from Bologna for London. Michael Holmes, the British Consul in Ancona, volunteered to drive them there. After a high speed, two hour drive on the autostrade, Alan and Brian arrived in Bologna just in time to board the plane. There was a strange sense of unreality at seeing Christine's face on the front pages of the British newspapers given out on the plane.

British Airways staff treated them with great kindness and consideration. At Heathrow, they were met by Jeanne Bell and other EDA friends who had flown down from Edinburgh. One of them was Rev. Andrew McLellan. In a talk given on the BBC Radio 2 programme 'Pause for Thought', he described that day.

'The journey by plane from Edinburgh to London takes about an hour, and I'll never forget it. I had no plan to go to London that day – until word came that Alan was arriving at Heathrow. It was only the day before that his wife Christine had been killed. They had been together on a mercy mission to Sarajevo. They had delivered their cargo of medicines, blankets and food, and they were driving out of the city when it happened. "Snipers' Alley" is the name the journalists have given to that particular street in Sarajevo. As Christine's truck made its way through the rubble, one more bullet found its mark.

I'm part of the small aid organization they were with in Bosnia. Edinburgh Direct Aid was founded last year by two friends of mine, and I've been proud to be involved with them. I think we always knew something like this might happen, but when it does, it is much more terrible than you expect. Alan had been in the truck in front of Christine: the least we could do was to be at the airport when he arrived.

There was a press conference. I suppose thirty journalists were there, because Christine's death had been headline news the day before. It must have been a fearful ordeal for Alan, especially as he had been reunited with his two children only minutes before. I was impressed with the sensitivity of the reporters, but they had to get their story. "Tell us," they asked, "was it your religious convictions that took you to Sarajevo?" "Yes," Alan replied, "The words of the Bible are, 'Love your neighbour'. We cannot stand back when this is happening to our neighbours". He and his wife had the courage and conviction to do what many of us know should be done but leave to others; and the world is nobler and better because of them.

To this day no-one knows anything about the sniper who fired the bullet that killed Christine Witcutt. It is difficult to try to see inside the mind of the killer of a defenceless retired schoolteacher who is trying to bring relief and healing to a city of destruction. What would you feel if you cradled your wife's dead body in the streets of Sarajevo? I could not guess what Alan would say in reply to the journalist who asked him, "What do you think of the people who shot your wife?" And I cried when with great humanity and dignity and faith he replied, "I'm trying to forgive them."

For the family, the next weeks were like a nightmare from which you can't wake up. The onslaught of the press and electronic news media was relentless. Alan was interviewed several times a day. There was an almost unbearable uncertainty about the date of the funeral. Christine's body had been flown to Italy on the same Hercules that carried Alan and Brian, but there were bureaucratic obstacles that took time to overcome, associated with transporting a body between countries. There seemed to be no mechanism for registering the death officially, which threatened to cause insuperable difficulties with processing all the paperwork. Finally, everything was resolved, and funeral arrangements were made for July 14th. Denis and the rest of the EDA party returned to Edinburgh on July 13th, just in time for the funeral.

It was dark and rainy as the mourners crowded into the chapel of Mortonhall Crematorium. Christine would have approved of the simple, elegant modernism of Sir Basil Spence's design. The press attended in large numbers, and BBC Television, with permission from the family, video-taped the service discreetly from the back. Flowers were sent by CNN, and one beautiful bouquet said simply 'From the People of Sarajevo.'

Christine had one final journey to make. On a sunny day in late July, Alan, Paul, Julie and Elspeth travelled to Glencoe and climbed the steep northern side of the glen. On a little plateau on Christine's beloved Aonach Eagach ridge, with a panoramic view of the magnificent scenery of Argyll, the family scattered her ashes, planted some heather, built a little cairn and scratched Christine's name on a stone to mark the spot. The wanderer had come home, to peace.

Elspeth found the following lines in Ewan MacColl's poem, 'The Joy of Living':

> Take me to some high place of heather, rock and ling,
> Scatter my dust and ashes, feed me to the wind,
> So that I will be part of all that you see,
> The air you are breathing –
> I'll be part of the curlew's cry and the soaring hawk,
> The blue milkwort and the sundew hung with diamonds:
> I'll be riding the gentle wind that blows through your hair,
> Reminding you how we shared in the joy of living.

Out of consideration for Julie and Paul, Alan does not intend to return to the war zone, but he has already been back to Croatia to bring back one of EDA's trucks. The work will continue as long as there is a need. A fund has been set up in Christine's memory, to help rebuild the Kosovo hospital in Sarajevo after the war is over.

Christine's contribution to the people of Bosnia was recognised on 6th November 1993, when she was the unanimous choice of the selection committee for the Sunday Mail's 1993 'Great Scot of the Year' award.

At the time of writing, Denis Rutovitz and Jeanne Bell are heading back to Sarajevo with another convoy of relief supplies. Denis's words, eloquent and passionate, make a fitting ending to this story. We are sure that Christine would agree. Somebody must *still* do something!

'For all of EDA the event was traumatic, numbing. Christine had gone to Bosnia knowing the risks and willing to face them because she believed that what she was doing was absolutely right, had to be done despite the risks. To turn away as a result of her death would be to say that it was all a mistake, and that we – and she – didn't really mean it. Nothing could be further from the truth: Christine certainly meant it.

EDA remembers and honours Christine in many ways, but the most important is in carrying on. And we want everyone to join us – not out in Bosnia, but in making the statement that we are trying to make by going there: namely that the killing and the expulsions and the rapes and the indignities and brutality of all sorts has to stop. That these people are part of our world – part of mankind, part of our history, part of our holidays, part of our Europe. That we may be glad of what our government has done so far, but we do want to say loud and strong to national leaders everywhere, that what has been done is not enough. That nothing can be enough, until the killing stops, and the Bosnians and Croatians (and Serbs too) can go back to the towns and villages from which they have been expelled, and can rebuild their lives and their homes, their schools, their hospitals, their churches and their mosques in safety and security. That is Christine's message.'

Appendix

Historical Background to the Yugoslav Conflict

The idea of Yugoslavia

After the horrors of 'ethnic cleansing', Yugoslavia, the land of the South Slavs, is unlikely ever to exist again as a single state. If this seems tragic, it is instructive to recognize that no such state existed in history until after the First World War. We may justly grieve for the innocent victims of this ghastly war, but we need to understand the historical realities of the region before we weep for the Yugoslav state. At no time during its brief existence have its people been able to set aside their ethnic differences and truly desire its continued survival as a united state. On the contrary, it has always been torn by destructive forces which are the direct result of the diverse histories of its peoples.

Based on the close similarities of the languages spoken by the various peoples of the region, nineteenth century intellectuals developed the idea that the South Slavs were a single people who should be gathered together in a single state. In 1917, in the midst of the terrible destruction of the First World War, the Serbian government-in-exile on the island of Corfu and a (non-elected) group of prominent Croats and Slovenes signed a declaration declaring the determination of the Serbian, Croatian and Slovene peoples to establish a united, independent, democratic kingdom, free of all foreign control. The Montenegrins, who consider themselves Serbs, also signed the declaration four weeks later. The new state – the first 'Yugoslavia' in history – was proclaimed on 1st December, 1918.

Yugoslavia was in trouble from the very beginning. Assembled from the wreckage of the Austro-Hungarian and Ottoman empires, its various regions had different histories, different religions, languages more distinct than the intellectuals claimed, even different alphabets.

The second Yugoslavia also arose from the ashes of war, and survived for 46 years under the iron hand of Tito's communists, only to disintegrate when the demise of Soviet communism set its people free to fight their ancient battles unhampered by Russian interventionism.

The history of Yugoslavia is an incredibly complex, multi-stranded web of migrations and invasions, empires and nations, religions and heresies, which together make a tragic, yet fascinating, story. This short appendix can only scratch its surface, sketching the broad outlines of a saga which covers 2,500 years.

Illyrians and Romans

During the first millennium BC, the lands we now think of as Yugoslavia were called Illyria. Its people are thought to have been of Celtic race, and were renowned as great seafarers. Illyria fought against Roman domination for 250 years. Defeated at last, Illyria became a Roman province in 168 BC, although the Dalmatians, an Illyrian tribe, held out until 46 BC. Though robbed of their independence, the Illyrians prospered under the Roman Empire. The best troops in the Roman army were Illyrians, as were the emperors Diocletian, Constantine and, probably, Justinian.

Memories of the long Illyrian resistance to Rome live on in local folk legends, two thousand years later. The idea of Illyria continues to hold great emotional appeal to many people, right up to the present day. In 1809, Napoleon combined the territories of Slovenia and Dalmatia to form what he chose to call the Illyrian Provinces. The nineteenth century creators of the Yugoslav idea called themselves at first the Illyrian Movement. Present day Albanians contend that they are the direct descendants of the Illyrians, and their primitive Indo-European language seems to support that belief. This claim has always been threatening to the Serbs, who fear that it may lead to territorial claims.

Christian Rome and Byzantium

Constantine was the first Roman emperor to become a Christian, and was responsible in 330 AD for moving the capital from Rome to Byzantium, a Greek city on the eastern frontier, which was better positioned to defend the empire from the hordes of barbarians constantly pressing westwards. Constantine's actions had momentous consequences that he certainly had never intended. He founded a new empire, instead of simply a new capital for the old empire. He also created a new eastern church, which ultimately came into acute conflict with the old Church in the west.

Unable to breach the defences of Byzantium, the Germanic invaders bypassed it, and fell instead on old Rome. The Western Empire soon crumbled and collapsed under their unrelenting pressure, while the eastern

Byzantine Empire stood for another eleven centuries. Although the differences in beliefs and ritual between the eastern and western branches of the church were relatively minor, political disputes combined with doctrinal differences to create a schism between the Roman Catholic and Orthodox churches in 1054 which has never been healed. The savage conquest of Constantinople by Catholic crusaders in 1204 left a legacy of undying hatred, making reconciliation impossible. This had disastrous long term consequences. The Byzantine/Orthodox and the Roman spheres of influence met and overlapped in what is now Bosnia, setting the scene for ferocious conflicts which are still continuing today.

The arrival of the Slavs

The original homeland of the Slavs lay north and east of the Carpathian mountains. During the sixth and seventh centuries they crossed the Danube and proceeded to settle and colonise the land that they conquered. In the north they expanded westwards to reach the Baltic coast of Germany, while in the south they pushed south and east into Yugoslavia, Greece, Albania and Asia Minor. The three major tribal divisions of the South Slavs into Croats, Serbs and Bulgarians and the territories they occupy to this day were established by the end of the ninth century. (Disputes between Serbs, Bulgarians and Greeks over the territory of Macedonia have triggered many wars in the past, and may well lead to an expanded conflict in the Balkans today.)

The Slovenes, a much smaller tribe, established a free Slovene state under Franko Samo which lasted from 623 to 658. The restoration of an independent Slovenia in 1991 after over 1300 years of submersion in other states as a more or less invisible minority, identifiable only by its language, is a striking example of how long and strongly the sense of individual tribal nationality has survived among the Slavs, retaining the power to influence later political actions and structures.

In due course, the South Slav tribes were converted to Christianity. The Croats and Slovenes became Roman Catholic, while the Serbs, falling under the influence of Byzantium, accepted the Orthodox religion and eventually were allowed to set up their own self-governing Serbian Orthodox Church.

A common Slavonic language was used throughout the Balkan peninsula, but no system of writing had yet been developed. Byzantine missionaries created two Slavonic alphabets (called Glagolitic and Cyrillic). To the Roman and Byzantine churches, the Slavonic language was too barbarous for use in divine service. Only Greek, Latin or Hebrew were considered appropriate. In Croatia, the Slav peasantry fought tenaciously for the right to hold services in their own language. After a struggle which went on for centuries, the Roman Catholic church was ultimately able to suppress the use of Slavonic and Glagolitic, but only after much bloodshed and brutality. Croats today use our familiar Latin alphabet.

The Orthodox church, on the other hand, eventually accepted both the Slavonic language and the Cyrillic alphabet. As a result, Cyrillic is now universally used in Serbia, as it is in Russia, Bulgaria and Macedonia. Serbs living in Croatia were quite happy using the Latin alphabet, until the newly-independent Croats decided to suppress the Cyrillic alphabet, creating yet another source of contention between Croats and Serbs.

The Bosnian heretics

One reason why the church opposed the use of Glagolitic was its fear of heresy. In the early centuries of Christianity, philosophers wrestled with the novel concepts and apparent paradoxes of Christian dogma. In consequence, the church was constantly bombarded by new ideas which threatened to tear it apart. Threatened by one such dispute over the divinity of Christ, Emperor Constantine summoned a general council of the church to meet in Nicaea in 325, to define a standard set of beliefs which church members would be compelled to accept on penalty of exile. Any idea not approved by the church was considered a heresy. Since heresies challenged the authority of the priesthood and the stability of the church, they were suppressed, often savagely.

One great heresy was founded by a Persian mystic named Mani in the third century and spread rapidly throughout the Mediterranean region. The Manichaeans believed that God, being perfect, had created only the world of the spirit, while the material world, being corruptible, had been created by an evil God (Satan or Lucifer). Manichaeans rejected the Old Testament entirely, and denied the Incarnation of Christ, since how could God have a body, if all bodies were created by Satan? They further preached that having babies simply added to the total amount of evil in the world, and that prostitution was therefore preferable to motherhood. The Manichaeans, who favoured a simple style of worship, made many converts and by the twelfth century had churches in Constantinople, Rumania, Bulgaria, Bosnia and Dalmatia, as well as considerable penetration in Italy and the south of France. The Christian church tried desperately to eradicate this heresy, which undermined the basic tenets of Christian faith and encouraged what the church saw as depraved behaviour.

Before the Turkish conquest, the majority of Bosnians belonged to a Manichaean sect known as Bogomils. Consistent with the Manichaean tradition, the Bogomils rejected the priesthood, the extravagant trappings and the worship of images and relics characteristic of both the Roman and

Orthodox churches. Members of the Bosnian church were perceived by both Croats and Serbs as wicked heretics.

Islam, the Crusades and the fall of Byzantium

In 610 AD, the prophet Mohammed received a call from God (Allah) to preach a new message of obedience to God's will. This was the beginning of an historical force which still has enormous, and growing, influence on the affairs of the world. In *A History of Europe,* Belgian historian Henri Pirenne wrote : 'In the whole history of the world there has been nothing comparable, in the universal and immediate nature of its consequences, with the expansion of Islam in the seventh century. The overwhelming rapidity of its propagation was no less surprising than the immensity of its conquests.' Only eighty years after the death of Mohammed in 632, the Muslims had overthrown the Persian Empire and conquered the Byzantine provinces of Syria, Egypt, North Africa and Spain.

The conquest of Sicily in 902 was the last advance of Islam in western Europe. Soon after began the Christian counter-attack. Severely weakened by defeats at the hands of, among others, the Croats, Serbs and Sicilian Normans, the Byzantine emperor appealed to the Pope in 1071 for help to recover land lost to the Seljuk Turks, and to protect the empire from further losses. The First Crusade was finally proclaimed in 1095, with the prime objective of recapturing Jerusalem and the holy places of Palestine from the Muslims who had held them since 638. Jerusalem was regained in 1099, but lost again. The Second and Third Crusades, also directed against the Turks, were total failures.

The Fourth Crusade in 1202-4 took a very different twist. The crusaders had contracted with the Venetians to transport them to the Holy Land, but did not have enough funds to pay for the chartered ships and crews. The Venetians, who were in savage competition with the Byzantines for control of the shipping trade in the eastern Mediterranean, persuaded the crusaders to attack Christian Constantinople before continuing to Syria. Constantinople was sacked, many of its citizens were massacred and vast amounts of loot, as well as priceless holy relics, were seized. A short-lived Latin Empire was founded in Constantinople.

Greek rule was restored in 1261, but the Byzantine Empire had been disastrously weakened and never recovered. Most of its European possessions had been lost. Greece had been retained by the Latins. The Serbs and the Bulgarians had established their own Balkan kingdoms free of Byzantine control.

Three centuries earlier, the South Slavs had already become strong enough to threaten Constantinople. In 1014, Emperor Basil II felt obliged to destroy a powerful confederation of Macedonians and Serbs, led by the

Macedonian prince Samuil. It is recorded that Basil ordered 14,000 Slav prisoners to be blinded, leaving one eye to every hundredth man to guide his comrades home. (Atrocities committed by Christian against Christian are not new in the Balkans.) After the restoration of the Byzantine Empire in 1261, the Serbs continued their pressure and it was clear that they intended to capture Constantinople.

During the eleventh century, the Seljuk Turks crossed from Europe into Asia Minor, and established a Turkish presence in Anatolia. Early in the thirteenth century, they were joined by the Ottoman Turks, who had fled south-westwards from western Turkestan to escape the hordes of Genghiz Khan. When the Seljuk empire disintegrated in the thirteenth century, the Ottoman Turks rose to dominate the remaining fragments. Weak, and threatened on their European borders, the Byzantines were unable to resist the Turkish expansion westwards.

By this time, the empire was but a shrunken shadow of its former glory, and was constantly torn by internal unrest. This weakness left the Turks free to nibble away at the imperial lands, while simultaneously providing military support to the Byzantines against their Christian enemies. In the 1340's, Ottoman forces were invited into Europe as mercenaries during one of the constant power struggles for the imperial throne. In 1354, they were allowed to cross the Straits and settle in Thrace to protect the empire from the challenge of the Serbs. A strange relationship had evolved between Turks and Byzantines. Intermarriage was quite common. Turkish troops assisted the Emperor on frequent occasions. Byzantine princes and statesmen accompanied Turkish armies into battle. Throughout all of this, the Turks continued to seize Byzantine cities and territories in both Europe and Asia Minor.

To understand this, it is important to realize that the Fourth Crusade had done more than simply damage the economic and military power of Constantinople. It had also established irrevocably in the hearts and minds of Orthodox believers (including Greeks, Serbs and Russians) the conviction that the west was *evil*. This secular act of banditry therefore reinforced the long-standing negative attitudes towards the western church, caused by the religious schism between the two churches. This belief in the inherent evilness of the west can readily be perceived in the rhetoric of the Russian communists during the Cold War. Many Byzantines preferred to surrender to the Turks than to appeal for help to the hated westerners and come under Roman Catholic rule.

Finally, the exhausted empire could hold out no more and Constantinople fell to Sultan Mohammed II in 1453. The last of the Greek emperors was killed in the battle, and the famous church of St. Sophia was looted of its treasures and converted to a mosque. Europe was now at the mercy of the Turks.

The medieval Serbian empire

The tribal people who were to become the Serbs settled in the southern portion of Yugoslavia, and founded the Serbian states of Zeta (roughly equivalent to today's Montenegro) and Raška (in the Ibar valley of southern Serbia). Converted to Christianity by Orthodox missionaries, the Serbs modelled their religious, cultural and political development on the Byzantine example.

The princes of the Nemanja dynasty were successful in uniting several small Serbian states in Montenegro and Hercegovina with their own territory of Raška, to create the first Serbian kingdom. Under the Nemanjas, the Serbs built ties with the west, threw off the rule of the Byzantines and established the independent Serbian Orthodox Church. Tsar Stefan Dušan the Mighty, the greatest of the Nemanjas, assembled an empire which included Serbia, Montenegro, Albania, Macedonia, much of Dalmatia, and parts of Greece. He crowned himself 'Emperor and Autocrat of the Serbs and Greeks, the Bulgarians and the Albanians' in 1349. (Some authorities prefer 'Emperor of the Serbs and Romans'.) Dušan's ambition was to seize the imperial throne of the Byzantine Empire and throw the Turks back from Europe, but he died suddenly in 1355, just when success seemed within his grasp.

The Serbian aristocracy fell to feuding after the death of Tsar Dušan, and his extensive empire quickly shattered into many independent principalities, which were picked off one by one by the Turks. But the Serbs have never ceased to yearn for the great era of the medieval Serbian Empire, remembering it throughout the long centuries of subjection to the Turks in epic sagas and ballads, passed from generation to generation by word of mouth. Probably the most potent of the memories thus preserved for the Serbs is of the Battle of Kosovo in 1389, but that is part of the next chapter of our history.

The fall of Serbia

The sudden death of Stefan Dušan in 1355 created a power vacuum in the Balkans which the Turks were quick to fill. Leaving Constantinople untouched, but surrounded by Turkish territory, the Ottomans captured Adrianople in 1361, then moved on into Bulgaria and Macedonia. Sofia fell in 1385 and Tirnovo in 1393. It was nearly 500 years before Bulgaria recovered its independence.

The Serbs too had to face the rampant power of the Turks. Easily defeating a Serbian attempt in 1371 to drive them out of Adrianople, the Turks pushed on into Macedonia. A coalition of northern Serbs and

Bosnians was able to defeat the Turks at Plocnik in 1386, but with disastrous consequences. The Turkish Sultan Murad returned with a large army, and met the Serbian forces at Kosovo on 28 June, 1389. The Serbs were defeated, and their leader, Prince Lazar, killed. Serbia was never again strong enough to challenge the Turks in the field, and was forced to accept Turkish overlordship.

The defeat of Kosovo became the subject of heroic and tragic folk ballads and is deeply engrained in the hearts of the Serbian people. The land of Kosovo itself is sacred soil for the Serbs, and the need to redeem it from alien occupation has been the Serbian 'Holy Grail' for over 600 years. (This lies at the heart of the Serbs' savage abuse of the Albanian Muslims of Kosovo, and their hatred of Muslims in general.)

Another seventy years were to pass before the final collapse of Serbia. The Turks turned their attentions next to Hungary, defeating them decisively in 1396. In 1402, the Turks had to pull back from Europe to Asia Minor to repel Tamerlane's Mongol hordes, granting a temporary respite to both the Serbs and the Byzantines. In 1453, Constantinople finally fell to the Turkish besiegers. The city might have been saved by an alliance with the Latin Christians. But the Byzantines hated the west more than they feared the Turks, and did not ask for help. The Serbs were to follow their example a few years later.

The last ruler of Serbia, Djordje Branković, having lost Belgrade to the Hungarians, built as his new capital the fortified city of Smederevo. It was captured by a huge army of Turks in 1439, but liberated soon after by the Hungarians. Djordje Branković had his lands and his fortress restored to him. But not for long. The end of the Serbian state, squeezed between Hungary and Turkey was inevitable. In 1459, the Orthodox defenders of Smederevo opened its gates to the Turks, rather than submit to the Catholic Hungarians. Serbia ceased to exist as a state. Its people were delivered into centuries of brutal oppression under the Ottoman yoke.

Bosnia and Hercegovina

Located between the Serbs to the south, the Croats, Slovenes and Austrians to the north and west and the Hungarians to the east, Bosnia's situation has always been difficult. Each of its neighbours has seen Bosnia as territory to be annexed, rather than as an independent state whose integrity should be respected. Its western regions have at times been part of Croatia, while much of eastern and central Bosnia has been incorporated into various Serbian states or empires.

As in other medieval states, power struggles between rival nobles were common, and Bosnia was frequently embroiled in civil war. Turkish mercenaries were used on occasion in these disputes, giving the Turks a foothold in the land. The Bosnians made territorial gains in the aftermath of the fall of Serbia, but the kingdom was surrendered to the Turks in 1463, only four years later. Its last king, Stefan Tomasević, had appealed to the Hungarians for help and refused to pay tribute to the Sultan. Mohammed II, conqueror of Constantinople, led his troops in person. Stefan was captured and offered his life if he would order his commanders to surrender their fortresses. He complied, and Bosnia fell with barely a blow struck in its defence. The Sultan reneged on his word, and Stefan was executed.

Long caught between the Orthodoxy of the Serbs and the Catholicism of the Croats and Hungarians, Bosnians had been subjected for centuries to the horrors of religious wars and sold into slavery by the traders of Ragusa. After the conquest, Bogomil Bosnians generally found Islam preferable to either Catholic or Orthodox Christianity, and were happy to embrace the Muslim faith. Nobles who converted acquired Turkish titles and were allowed to keep their lands. Most Catholic and Orthodox Bosnians remained Christian. Those who became Muslims were spared the tribute demanded of Christians under Turkish rule. The Christians were reduced to serfdom, and forced to work the fields of the Muslim nobles.

Life under the Turks

The administrative systems of the Ottoman state, both military and civil, were founded on the institution of slavery. The heir to the throne was always borne by a member of the Sultan's harem. Since the harem was made up of slaves, mostly Christian-born, each new Sultan was always half-slave.

The highest officials of the Ottoman empire were also slaves, recruited from the children of its Christian subjects. These boys were specially selected, converted to Islam, and trained for years to fill their roles. The elite troops of the Ottoman army, known as the janissaries, were made up exclusively of these Christian levies. By the sixteenth century, the janissaries were over 100,000 strong, and were unmatched by any fighting force in Europe. (Later, the levy of Christian boys was ended, and the janissaries became simply a corps of picked men.)

In the conquered Slav territories, the native aristocracy was replaced by Turks, lost their lands and disappeared as a class. The population as a whole was regarded by the Turks as little more than human cattle, to be disposed of without further consideration. Despite this lowly status, the common people probably found the initial years of Ottoman rule less harsh than the native feudalism that it replaced. Justice was indeed harsh and brutal, but no more so than it had been under the Serbs or the Byzantines. The Ottoman Empire was founded on the basis of religion rather than race. All those who accepted Islam were considered Turks. All subjects were free to remain Christian, although they were obliged to pay an annual head-tax, and to submit to the levy on their sons. With the exception of Bosnia and Hercegovina, most Slavs remained Christian during the centuries of Turkish rule.

In Bosnia, things were better at first, at least for the new Muslims. The conversion of so many Bosnians to Islam meant that Bosnia was regarded more favourably by the Ottoman empire than were the Christian subject states. Few ethnic Turks actually took up permanent residence in the conquered Balkan territories. Most stayed only temporarily for the duration of their tours of duty in the military or civil service. As a result, even in Bosnia, the population is still overwhelmingly Slav today, although Bosnian Muslims consider themselves Turks.

Ottoman power began to decline early in the seventeenth century. The empire had now become too large for its highly centralised administrative system to control efficiently. As its central authority weakened, many Turkish officials in the subject territories exploited their new independence and became corrupt and oppressive. The once disciplined janissaries stooped to extortion, slaughter and torture, reinforcing the Serb contention that 'a Serb turned Turk is worse than a Turk'. The lot of the subject peoples, in Bosnia as elsewhere, became harsh indeed. Early in the eighteenth century, Sultan Selim III attempted to dismantle the corps of janissaries, leading to a series of destructive revolts, which further weakened the empire.

With their national spirit sustained by the Orthodox church and the epic ballads of their glorious history, the Serbs fought an endless guerrilla war against the Turks. Operating from the forests and mountains, bands of outlaws, known as hajduks, harassed the Turks, robbing their caravans and distributing the proceeds to the villagers who sustained them through the winter. Captured hajduks were put to death most brutally. The Turks used gypsy executioners, skilled in the art of impaling a man on a sharp stake, so that it would enter his groin and leave at his shoulder without puncturing a vital organ as it passed through his body. Death was slow and agonizing.

The famous Sultan Suleiman the Magnificent captured Belgrade from the Hungarians in 1521, and besieged Vienna unsuccessfully in 1532. The Ottomans tried again in 1683, when Vienna was saved by the heroism of its garrison and the timely arrival of help from the King of Poland. Austria retaliated by mounting a massive counter-offensive and penetrated deep into Serbia, whereupon the Serbs rose in support. Fearing reprisals when the Austrians withdrew in 1690, tens of thousands of Serbs migrated northwards from Kosovo to the region of southern Hungary now known as the Vojvodina, creating a large minority of Serbs among the Magyars of this vast fertile plain. When the Turks returned, they repopulated southern Serbia, particularly the plains of Kosovo, with Muslim Albanians.

(The Vojvodina became part of Yugoslavia in 1920 and is now part of

Serbia. Its large Magyar population may well become a cause of hostilities between Serbia and Hungary. Tito's communist regime made Kosovo a semi-autonomous province of Yugoslavia, in recognition of its 80% Albanian Muslim majority, and denied Serbs the right to settle there. The Serbs now have total control of Kosovo and, still seeking revenge for their historic defeat in 1389, have already deprived its Muslim population of many basic civil rights, including education. Worse is probably to come.)

Croatia, Slovenia, Hungary and Austria

Croatia and Slovenia were spared the misery of Turkish rule, but had to accept the domination of their Christian neighbours for many centuries. Slovenia, converted to Roman Catholicism by the Franks in the eighth and ninth centuries, was incorporated into the Holy Roman Empire during the tenth century, and later absorbed by the Habsburg empire, where the Slovenes seemed quite content to remain until the First World War destroyed their Austrian protectors and catapulted them into the new Kingdom of Serbs, Croats and Slovenes. (Declaring their independence from Yugoslavia only hours after Croatia in 1991, they were also the lucky ones. They were buffered from the centralism of the Serbs by the equally separatist Croats, and achieved their freedom with the loss of fewer than 100 Slovene lives in the course of their short engagement with the Yugoslav People's Army.)

Converted to Christianity by the Latin inhabitants of Dalmatia, the Croats were the first of the South Slavs to establish an independent kingdom. Lying on the dividing line between the Frankish and Byzantine empires, the Croatian state endured from 925 to 1102, when disputes over the succession led Croatia's nobles to offer the crown of Croatia, Slavonia and Dalmatia to the king of Hungary. Dalmatia was later lost to the Venetians. Croatia found itself on the front line between Venice, Hungary and the Ottoman empire. A constant stream of Slav refugees from Turkish oppression flowed in, introducing significant minorities with different religions and histories.

The Croats turned to the Austrian Habsburg dynasty to take over the throne in 1527, after the devastating defeat of the Hungarian armies by the Turks the previous year left most of Hungary under Turkish rule for 150 years. As the Ottoman empire gradually retreated, the Habsburgs created a Military Frontier territory out of recaptured Croatian and Hungarian lands instead of restoring them to Croatian control. Many of the Serbian refugees were resettled there by the Habsburgs to defend their lands from the still dangerous Turks. The Serbs were allowed to retain their Orthodox religion and Cyrillic alphabet. This created a large Serbian minority in Croatia which led to much bloodshed in later years.

(All over the world, imperialism has resulted in the mingling of diverse peoples and the creation of national boundaries which take no account of the ethnic mix within them, sowing the seeds of many future conflicts. This is one of the fundamental causes of the Yugoslav conflict.)

Liberation and betrayal

The first half of the nineteenth century was a tumultuous period in Europe. The French and American revolutions had shown that the old regimes were vulnerable. Napoleon was about to unleash his French legions in a massive effort to rule the world. The Ottoman empire was in chaos, being attacked from within by the now uncontrollable janissaries, and under constant pressure from Austria and Russia. Aware that the janissaries intended to massacre several hundred Serbian leaders, the Serbs were forced to make a bid for freedom. Under the leadership of Djordje Petrović, known as Black Djordje or Karadjordje, a pig farmer who had served in the Austrian army, Serbian fighters drove the Turks out of Serbia by 1810. When Napoleon attacked Russia in 1812, the Russians were obliged to make peace with the Turks, who then returned in force to Serbia, recapturing Belgrade in 1813. Karadjordje fled to Austria.

In reprisal for the Serbian uprising, the Turks instituted a brutal reign of terror, leaving the Serbs no alternative but to rebel again. Their leader this time was Milos Obrenović, whose half brother had allegedly been poisoned by Karadjordje in 1810. Obrenović was a crafty and devious diplomat. In order to win favour, he had Karadjordje murdered and sent his head to the Sultan. (The vicious rivalry of the Karadjordjević and Obrenović families carried on until the end of the Yugoslav monarchy shortly after the Second World War.) Russia, victorious over Napoleon, brought diplomatic pressure to bear on the Turks, and in 1830 Serbia was recognised as an autonomous principality under Milos Obrenović, though still tributary to the Sultan.

Serbia was now embarked on a path which would lead to full independence as a democratic monarchy under the Karadjordjević dynasty in 1903, but many serious obstacles had to be overcome first. Serbians began to dream again of restoring their ancient boundaries and bringing all Serbs and Serb lands together once more.

Hungary rebelled against the rule of Vienna in the great revolutionary year of 1848. The Croats sided with the Austrians, but were returned to Magyar control in 1867. Croatia was to remain under the Hungarians until the destruction of the Austro-Hungarian Dual Monarchy in 1918.

In 1875 Bosnia rose in revolt over the extortionate and brutal practices of the Ottoman tax collectors. This triggered a period of great crisis over the whole Balkan region. The revolt spread to Bulgaria where, in reprisal, the Turks massacred 10,000 to 12,000 Bulgarians in 1876. Serbia and

Montenegro then entered the war, but were defeated by the Turks. Russia declared war on Turkey to aid its fellow Slavs, hoping to seize territory from the crumbling Ottoman empire. The Austrians agreed to remain neutral in the conflict, in return for the promise that Bosnia-Hercegovina would be ceded to Vienna. From this time on, Austria and Serbia were on a collision course towards disaster for both.

It had long been British policy to deny Russia access to the Mediterranean, which would have threatened Britain's communications with its empire in the east. To this end, Britain had allied itself with Turkey during the Crimean War twenty years earlier. Public outrage over the Bulgarian atrocities kept Britain out of the war this time, and the defeated Turks were forced to sign the Treaty of San Stefano in March, 1878. In its initial form, this treaty defined enormous changes in the Balkans. Serbia and Rumania achieved full independence from the Turks. A new, large Bulgaria was to be created, which would include most of Macedonia. Its prince would be tributary to the Sultan. The Russians would remain in occupation for two years. Turkish possessions in Europe would be reduced to disconnected fragments.

Britain and Austria were vehemently opposed to this expansion of Russian power in the Balkans. They convened an international conference in Berlin, and forced Russia to accept a drastically modified settlement. Macedonia was returned to the Turks, thwarting once again the long-standing Bulgarian yearning to possess this territory. Bulgaria itself was divided into two provinces, the northern to become an autonomous principality, initially under Russian supervision. The new southern province was placed under the direct control of the Turkish Sultan. Austria was allowed to occupy Bosnia and Hercegovina, although the Sultan still retained nominal sovereignty.

The road to World War I

By depriving Russia of almost all its war gains, the Berlin Congress achieved its objective of limiting Russian expansion in the Balkans. But its terms satisfied none of the former belligerents, and led directly to several Balkan wars, and indirectly to the First World War and the final destruction of the Habsburg and Ottoman empires.

Disputes soon erupted over Macedonia, with the Bulgarians defeating a Serbian attack in 1885. Restoration of the Karadjordjević line to the throne of Serbia in 1903 led to a rapprochement between Serbia and Bulgaria, which signed economic and cultural agreements and started discussing a political alliance.

Croatia and Bosnia-Hercegovina were both still in Habsburg hands. In Croatia and Dalmatia, the Habsburgs had intentionally provoked Croat-

Serb antagonism by favouring the minority Serbs over the Croats. Rioting between the two groups was common. Nevertheless, in 1903 they began to cooperate against their mutual oppressor, the Hungarians, with a Croat-Serb coalition winning a majority in the next elections to the Croatian parliament. The Habsburgs unwisely inflamed the situation by trying some fifty Croats and Serbs for treason, on trumped-up charges of conspiring to unite Croatia and Bosnia-Hercegovina with Serbia. Several assassination attempts were made against Magyar Governors in Croatia, in two cases by Bosnians.

Austria was very concerned about any expansion of Serbian power and, in response to the agreements between Serbia and Bulgaria, precipitated the so-called 'pig war' of 1906-7 by closing its borders to imports of Serbian livestock. Montenegro, always pro-Serbian, was still independent, having successfully resisted all Turkish attempts at conquest for several centuries because of its rugged mountainous terrain. Austria announced its intention to build a railway line through the border area between Serbia and Montenegro which would block the future union of the two Serb states.

In 1908, with the Ottoman empire distracted by the Young Turk Revolution, Austria seized the opportunity to officially annex Bosnia-Hercegovina. In Bosnia, the Habsburgs had again followed the policy of 'divide and rule', conciliating the Muslims at the expense of the Christian Serb and Croat majority. The Croats wanted to join Croatia, while the Serbs favoured union with Serbia. The Muslims mourned the departed Turks.

Annexation seemed to slam the door shut on the national aspirations of all three groups. It inflamed anti-Austrian passion in Serbia, which was disposed to challenge the mighty Habsburg empire. Russia supported the Serbs, but having recently suffered defeat at the hands of Japan, was not ready to fight. Although a major war was therefore averted, tensions between Austria and Serbia continued to rise, as Serbia pursued its independent political destiny in defiance of the Habsburgs' fury.

In 1912, a series of treaties linked Bulgaria, Serbia, Greece and Montenegro into the Balkan League, an alliance directed against the remaining European possessions of the Ottoman empire. The First Balkan War broke out in the summer of that year. The defeated Turks were left only a tiny area in Europe. Serbia captured northern Albania and achieved access to the Adriatic. Montenegro and Greece also made significant gains. Fearing that a Serbian port on the Adriatic would give the Russians access to the Mediterranean, the great powers once again thwarted the ambitions of the Balkan nations by creating a new Albanian state. Bulgaria refused Serbian demands to cede it additional Macedonian territory in compensation.

The Balkan League collapsed and the Second Balkan War erupted in June, 1913. Bulgaria attacked Serbia and Greece, which were joined by the

Rumanians and Turks. Bulgaria was quickly defeated, and lost territory to all four of its adversaries. Serbia and Greece divided Macedonia between them. Serbia and Montenegro took over the former Austrian buffer territory which had separated them, and established a common frontier. Serbia also tried desperately to hold on to its cherished access to the sea in Albania. The Austrians, backed by the German Kaiser, delivered an ultimatum to Serbia, giving them one week to evacuate their troops from Albania. The Serbs were forced to comply.

Serbian bitterness towards the Austrians was now combined with burgeoning self-confidence. Having doubled its size, thrown Turkey out of Europe and linked up with fellow Serbs in Macedonia and Montenegro, Serbia began to appear like a real threat to the Austro-Hungarian Dual Monarchy. Ironically, Archduke Franz Ferdinand, heir to the Habsburg throne, was well aware of the dangers of this situation. He favoured a radical solution, incorporating all the South Slavs into a single political unit which would have equal status with Austria and Hungary in a new Triple Monarchy. It is interesting to speculate what might have happened had he lived to assume power. His concept was opposed by the hard line 'hawks' in Budapest and Vienna, and equally by Croatian and Serbian nationalists. It was one of the latter who precipitated the First World War, which was to change the face of the world forever.

The Austrians were talking openly of a pre-emptive war against Serbia. Throughout the Habsburg lands, Slavs were being subjected to increasingly savage oppression. Bosnian Serbs were singled out for particularly severe treatment. In a very provocative move, Vienna decided to hold military manoeuvres in eastern Bosnia. The Archduke and his wife were to review the troops in Sarajevo on 28th June 1914, the anniversary of the Turkish defeat of Serbia in the Battle of Kosovo. A Bosnian Serb student shot and killed Franz Ferdinand, using weapons from the Serbian state arsenal. Austria demanded reparations from Serbia in terms so harsh that they were clearly expected to be rejected, giving Austria a pretext for punitive military action against Serbia. Serbia in fact was willing to comply almost completely. It appeared that the remaining points could be cleared up by negotiation. But Austria declared war, and was joined immediately by Germany and Turkey. As subjects of Austria-Hungary, the Croats, Slovenes and Bosnians were forced to fight on the side of the Central Powers. Russia, France and Britain, joined later by Italy, the United States and Rumania, came to the aid of Serbia. Over eight million men were to die during the next four years.

Serbia, although already exhausted from three years of constant warfare, did well in the first months of the World War. The Austrians invaded Serbia twice, but were thrown back. In October 1915, Bulgaria joined with German and Austrian forces and drove the Serbs back through Albania and on to the island of Corfu, where in 1917 the Serbian government-in-exile and the self-appointed Yugoslav Committee of Croats and Slovenes signed their historic agreement to establish a South Slav kingdom.

In the light of what was to happen later, it is important to recognize that the various parties to this agreement had different motives for signing it. The Yugoslav Committee was philosophically committed to the old 'Illyrian' ideal of a single state for all South Slavs where each of its peoples, divided and enslaved by foreign empires for centuries, would be free and equal and live together in peace and harmony. Serbia, on the other hand, was more interested in creating a 'Greater Serbia' and recovering its outlet to the Mediterranean than in uniting with Croats and Slovenes on equal terms. It also had doubts about the extent to which the Yugoslav Committee really represented the desires of the Croat and Slovene peoples. However, when the Bolshevik revolution took Russia out of the war, the Serbs realised that the balance of power in the region had changed. The United States had entered the war, and President Woodrow Wilson had distinctly pro-Yugoslav views. The Corfu Declaration was the result.

United at last

Under a secret treaty signed in London in 1915, Italy had been promised a major part of northern Dalmatia and other territories on the Adriatic mainly inhabited by South Slavs in return for entering the war on the Allied side. The Yugoslav Committee saw this as a serious threat to their objective of establishing a single state for all South Slavs, and wanted Serbian forces to oppose the Italian takeover. In the autumn of 1918, the Habsburg monarchy collapsed. Serbia now acceded to desperate pleas for help from the Croats and Slovenes, but was able to dictate the terms under which the union would take place. Finally, on 1st December 1918, the Kingdom of Serbs, Croats and Slovenes, the first united state of the South Slavs in history, was proclaimed. One Croatian voice alone spoke out against unification, warning that the mass of the people did not want this union. This was Stjepan Radić, the founder of the Croat People's Peasant Party. Indeed, at no time have the peoples of Yugoslavia ever been consulted about whether they wished to become part of a unified state. This status has on each occasion been forced upon them by military action or the decisions of unelected representatives.

The new kingdom was immediately involved in territorial disputes with the Italians, so Yugoslavia and Italy were therefore alienated from the beginning. Although the Versailles Peace Conference rejected the London Treaty, the final boundaries agreed between Italy and Yugoslavia in 1924 in fact left over half a million Croats and Slovenes under Italian rule until the end of the Second World War.

Yugoslavia's first king, Alexander Karadjordjević, a descendant of Black

Djordje Petrović, was of course a Serb. In its initial form, the country was called, not Yugoslavia, but 'the Kingdom of the Serbs, Croats and Slovenes', which ignored the Albanians, Macedonians, Hungarians, Montenegrins, Bosnians and Herzegovinians who also lived in their midst. The Serbs naturally assumed that they had finally achieved the 'Greater Serbia' of their dreams, and that it was their historic destiny to rule their fellow Slavs. Many of their compatriots felt that they had simply exchanged one foreign oppressor for another. The Croatians soon realised the accuracy of Radić's warnings, when they found that they had even less political and cultural autonomy than they had had under the Habsburgs. From then on, conveniently forgetting the terms of union they had agreed to, Croats stubbornly resisted the centralism of Serbian control.

The economic upheavals of the post-war period and the subsequent great depression took place in a land which had never known democracy. Suppressed in feudal serfdom for centuries and frozen in a kind of medieval 'time warp', the South Slavs had been bypassed by the great movements of enlightenment which had swept western Europe since the sixteenth century. How could they be expected to play the elegant games of constitutional democracy when they had never had a chance to learn the rules?

A large Communist Party developed, but was soon banned. The Serbian Radical Party and the Croatian Peasant Party were regionally rather than nationally based. The Serbs wanted a monarchy under Serb-dominated central control. The Croats initially wanted a loose federation, preferably a republic, but later demanded such a degree of devolution to the provinces that each would have controlled its own army.

Such total disagreement on the constitutional form of the state – centralised or federated, monarchy or republic – ultimately made it impossible to maintain even a facade of democratic government. King Alexander was forced to suspend the constitution and assume dictatorial powers with all the trappings of a police state. Introducing even more rigorous centralisation, Alexander now rejected the idea of a kingdom of three different nations, and changed the name of his country to 'the Kingdom of Yugoslavia', the first state to bear the name Yugoslavia. In reality, the country fragmented even more under his authoritarian rule, which ended when he was assassinated in Marseilles in 1934. The killer was a Macedonian terrorist acting on behalf of the Croatian Ustaše, a fascist terrorist organization which was dedicated to the destruction of Yugoslavia as the only way to achieve Croatian independence. A few years later, the Ustaše was to play an horrific role in the Second World War.

Alexander's cousin, Prince Paul, was appointed as regent to govern during the minority of King Peter, then aged eleven. Throughout his regency, he steadfastly refused to allow a return to democratic government, and resisted Croat demands for devolution until 26th August 1939, when Croatia was granted a limited degree of autonomy. This stirred up Serbian resentment, and destroyed the nascent friendship which had begun to develop while Serbs and Croats both felt equally oppressed by Paul's autocratic dictatorship.

The destruction of the first Yugoslavia

When the Second World War broke out in September 1939, Yugoslavia at first declared its neutrality. Under intense pressure from Hitler, on 25th March 1941 Prince Paul finally agreed to make Yugoslavia a non-belligerent member of the Axis Pact. Although Paul was denounced for having capitulated to Hitler, he had actually secured German agreement to respect the inviolability of Yugoslavia's borders and the assurance that Axis troops would not march through Yugoslav territory in their planned invasion of Greece. The Germans did not publish the clauses restraining their freedom of action, although they later appeared in full in the Yugoslav Official Gazette. The Serbs, outraged at the apparent capitulation, reacted immediately and with disastrous consequences. Prince Paul was overthrown by a Serbian military *coup d'état* on 27th March 1941. King Peter, not yet eighteen, was proclaimed King, amidst wild celebrations and anti-German demonstrations in the streets of Belgrade.

The new government quickly realised that Hitler would consider their *coup* as intolerable provocation. Trying desperately to back-pedal, they accepted the terms of Prince Paul's agreement with the Axis, but to no avail. Hitler flew into one of his insane rages and issued orders for the destruction of Yugoslavia, the attacks to be 'carried out with unmerciful harshness'. Hitler assumed that the Croats would come to the German side. German bombers attacked Belgrade without warning on 6th April 1941, even though it had been declared an open city. In the three-day air operation, seventeen thousand Yugoslavs were killed. All-out invasion by twenty-seven army and Panzer divisions followed swiftly, and the country fell ten days later.

Yugoslavia was now dismembered, as the Axis powers divided up their spoils. Germany annexed two-thirds of Slovenia. Italy got the rest of Slovenia, most of the Adriatic coast and islands, and Montenegro. Hungary acquired the Vojvodina and small areas of Slovenia and Croatia. Albania was awarded Kosovo, along with parts of Macedonia and Montenegro. The rest of Macedonia and parts of Serbia went to Bulgaria. The remaining territories were divided between two new states, Serbia and Croatia. The rump state of Serbia was treated as a conquered enemy, with a puppet government to maintain order and fight the resistance movements that sprang up immediately.

The Croats were treated as allies to be rewarded rather than enemies to be punished. Ante Pavelić, leader of the Ustaše, was made the Poglavnik or

Führer of Croatia. The Croatian crown was offered to, and accepted by, the Duke of Spoleto, second cousin of King Victor Emmanuel of Italy, a figurehead and spokesman of Mussolini's fascist regime. Croatia's territorial losses to Italy were compensated by the award of Bosnia-Hercegovina. As a German puppet state, it soon declared war on the Allies and the Soviet Union.

The Ustaše now embarked on a barbarous campaign of genocide against the Jews and the two million Serbs of the new Croatia. The Jews were killed or sent to concentration camps for extermination. Against the Serbs, the Ustaše strategy was simple: convert a third of them to Catholicism, expel a third to Serbia, and kill the rest. Tens of thousands were butchered in concentration camps. The populations of whole Serb villages were burned alive in their Orthodox churches. In this ghastly work, the Ustaše had the support of some senior members of the Croatian and Bosnian Catholic clergy, including the Archbishop of Sarajevo. Members of the Franciscan order actively participated in the massacres and forced conversions. Such was the hatred between the two Christian communities.

The Muslim population was treated by Pavelić's regime as long-lost Croat brothers. Some Muslims assisted the Ustaše in the slaughter, and eventually a special SS division was created for them. (The Hungarians, not to be outdone, killed at least 10,000 Serbs in the territories ceded to them. In the Albanian-annexed areas of Yugoslavia, the Albanian minority massacred Serbs with impunity.)

Estimates of the number of Serbs killed by the Croats during this period vary from 350,000 to over 1 million. News of the massacres appalled exiled Serbs. Blaming the whole Croat people along with the fanatical Ustaše, the Serbs swore that Yugoslavia could never be recreated unless a million Croats were slaughtered first. They overlooked the fact that the Serbs were equally savage in their massacres of Croats and Muslims.

Resistance and civil war

The full story of the Yugoslav resistance and the civil war which accompanied it is still the subject of dispute among historians. This was a period of great chaos, and all parties to the conflict made considerable use of misinformation and propaganda to assist them to achieve their own objectives.

Although the unprepared Yugoslav army had broken under the onslaught of the Axis forces, it was not totally destroyed. Many units took to the woods, taking their weapons with them, or hiding them in secret dumps. Taking the name Četniks, from the Serb guerrillas who in earlier centuries had valiantly resisted the Turks, these ex-army fighters were fanatically loyal to the Serbian monarchy and to the idea of a greater Serbia. Together with other Serbs who had been driven into the Bosnian mountains by the Ustaše's massacres, they began to carry out sabotage against German troops, installations and supplies. The Germans reacted to these incidents by executing Serbian civilian hostages, proclaiming that 100 Serbs would die for every German killed, and 50 for every one wounded. In Kragujevac, the old capital of Serbia in the days of Prince Miloš Obrenović, German soldiers shot 7,000 citizens, including 300 children and their teachers. The Četniks soon decided to pull back, in order not to provoke more reprisals against Serbs.

The Četniks were not the only group resisting the occupation. The Communist Party of Yugoslavia, although banned for years under the monarchy, had simply remained underground, all the while organising and planning for the eventual overthrow of the bourgeois state. Its Secretary-General, Josip Broz, later known as Tito, was a loyal Stalinist. Hitler and Stalin had a signed non-aggression pact. Tito's Croat Communists had followed the Moscow line by actively encouraging desertion from the Royalist army during the Axis invasion (adding yet another bone of contention between Serbs and Croats). Only when Germany attacked the USSR on 21st June 1941 did Tito throw his Communist fighters, later to be known as Partisans, into the fray against the occupying forces.

For a time, the royalist Četniks cooperated with the Communist Partisans in joint operations. Eventually the leader of the Četniks, Colonel (later General) Draža Mihailović, decided that the Partisans were a greater threat to his beloved Serbia than the Germans. Tito, in turn, realised that he would have to eliminate the Četniks if his plan to establish a Communist state in Yugoslavia were ever to succeed. Collaboration was impossible, when each was committed to destroying what the other was sworn to defend. The result was one of the bloodiest civil wars ever seen in Europe.

Partisans and Četniks fought each other, the occupying Axis forces and their quisling collaborators. The Partisans frequently betrayed Četniks to the Germans. As the war progressed, the Četniks' opposition to the Partisans led some of them into more and more direct collaboration with the Italians and, later, the Germans. Late in 1942, Tito was so concerned that the Četniks might defeat his Partisans that he made an offer to the Germans through direct negotiations. If the Germans would agree to a truce with the Partisans to allow Tito to concentrate on the destruction of the Četniks, the Partisans would fight on the German side to oppose any Allied landing on the Adriatic coast. Hitler rejected this proposal and launched an offensive against the Partisans that almost wiped them out.

Atrocities on all sides continued to be a major feature of the civil war. Those of the Četniks soon matched the Ustaše massacres of 1941. In one 1943 example, the Četniks attempted to exterminate the Muslims, Croats and pro-Partisan inhabitants in the Sanjak area between Serbia and Montenegro, perpetrating slaughter on an enormous scale. On their part, the Partisans killed great numbers of 'traitors', a term they applied to anyone who resisted their efforts to impose Communism by force, following a similar macabre arithmetic to that of the Nazis: ten anti-Communists for one Partisan death.

In the end, the Partisans prevailed. At Tito's request, Stalin diverted the Third Ukranian Army, which occupied the Serbian heartland while the Germans were withdrawing from the rest. Četniks who surrendered or were captured were slaughtered by the Partisans, as were thousands of Slovenes, Croats and other nationalities who were forcibly repatriated by the British from Carinthia to Yugoslavia at the end of the war. A coalition government was formed in March 1945, and the country was fully liberated from the Germans by May. Over 1.2 million Yugoslavs had died since 1941, a tremendous number of them killed by other Yugoslavs. Before the end of 1945, the Communists had abolished the monarchy, and the second Yugoslavia was born as a Federal People's Republic under the control of Marshall Tito. General Mihailović was tried as a collaborator and shot in July 1946.

Communist Yugoslavia

Tito's regime was generally perceived by westerners as a 'a kinder, gentler Communism', fundamentally benevolent, as opposed to the harsh and brutal oppression of Stalinism. The Yugoslav people were unique in the Communist world in that they were free to travel and work outside the country. While there is some truth in these perceptions, the reality is that the oppression of Tito's regime differed only in scale and not in quality from that of Stalin. Their revolution successful, the Communists proceeded to impose an iron control on the state and its peoples. With the suppression of free speech, no public debate or resolution of the horrors of the civil war was permitted. The trauma was never exorcised from the collective psyche of the people, but was simply frozen until the collapse of the Communist system allowed all the old hatreds to spring forth again.

Tito administered Yugoslavia as a federation of six Republics – Serbia, Croatia, Slovenia, Macedonia, Bosnia-Hercegovina and Montenegro – and two Autonomous Provinces, Vojvodina and Kosovo, all having their own Communist Party organisations, initially tightly controlled from Belgrade, but later gaining almost total local autonomy. Under the constitution, it was illegal for any republic to secede from the federation, notwithstanding the fact that they had never been asked whether they wanted to join.

The Communists had no desire to re-establish a Serb-dominated state. The decision to set up Vojvodina and Kosovo as autonomous provinces instead of incorporating them into Serbia was calculated to keep Serbian pride under control. The Serbs were compensated by giving them a disproportionate share of the privileged positions of power in the Croatian administration, while their presence in the police forces helped to keep Croatian nationalism in check.

The main objective of Tito's strategies for dealing with the nationalities issue seems to have been to keep the various ethnic groups feuding among themselves, instead of combining to resist the power of the Communist regime. The Serb, Croat and Muslim national groups identify themselves by their respective religions. Communism imposed an atheistic philosophy on all national groups which was alien to their histories and cultures, stifling the spiritual aspects of their lives. The prohibition of open debate and dialogue about Yugoslav history, politics and the bloody events of the civil war, turned the various groups inwards, nurturing their paranoia about their compatriots. The net result appears to have been a regression to a medieval state of barbarism, where members of other groups are considered as sub-human and can be slaughtered like animals.

Many fascinating accounts have been written about Tito's break with Stalin, but that is beyond the scope of this short history. Tito at first introduced strict Stalinist policies, but, recognising that this would destroy his country's economy, he successfully broke away from the direct control of the USSR. To ensure that his actions were not challenged from within, he had over 50,000 suspected Yugoslav Stalinists interned and tortured on the Adriatic island of Goli Otok.

The success of Tito's defiance confirmed his reputation as a national hero, strengthened Yugoslavia's sense of national identity for a time and bolstered the confidence and prestige of the Communists. Always afraid that the Soviet Union might invade Yugoslavia as it had Hungary and Czechoslovakia, Tito established arms dumps all over the country to facilitate an 'all peoples' defence system'. (Many of these weapons have now found their way into the hands of the various factions fighting each other today in the Yugoslav lands.) Only the American willingness to defend South Korea against Communist aggression may have stopped Stalin from invading Yugoslavia in 1951.

Tito was well aware of the powder keg of nationalist feelings that had to be contained. He suppressed all national rights, and attempted, with some success, to substitute the Yugoslav ideal. (In the long run, this strategy did not work any better for Tito than it had for King Alexander.) Work began in 1954 to define a common Serbo-Croatian language.

Economic development and industrialisation progressed during the 1950s and early 1960s, promising a better standard of living for the population, and the country experienced a decade of stability. As the economy began to flag in the 1960s, unrest reappeared among the various national groups. The Croats now insisted that Croatian should be treated as a separate tongue, while the Serbs demanded that Serbians in Croatia should be allowed to use the Cyrillic alphabet. Foreign currency earned by tourism and industry in Croatia and Slovenia, and sent home by Croatian workers abroad, was redistributed by the central government to pay for the development of the backward former Ottoman territories, including Serbia itself. The Croats greatly resented being taxed to support those whom they again saw as oppressors. 'End the plunder of Croatia' became their rallying cry. Croatian terrorists began to operate abroad. The Yugoslav Ambassador in Sweden was murdered. Planes were hijacked or blown up.

In response to this challenge, Tito doubled the amount of foreign exchange which each enterprise was allowed to retain from its earnings, and introduced a significant degree of decentralisation. The Constitution was amended, devolving substantial powers to the individual republics, and later giving them the right of veto inside the collective presidency. Foreign affairs, defence and economic planning were the only areas left under federal control. The disintegration of Yugoslavia had begun.

Kosovo, as always, was a trouble spot. Tito had at first tolerated, if not encouraged, harsh oppression of the Albanian population there. In 1966, the government admitted that its secret police had perpetrated horrible massacres against the Albanians in Kosovo. Many Serbs had joined the security service expressly for the opportunity to commit atrocities against the Albanians.

In the late sixties, he changed his tactics, and favoured the Albanians over the Serb minority. The 1974 Constitution significantly strengthened the local powers of both Autonomous Provinces. The fragmentation of the economy accelerated. All the essential services were divided into eight separate authorities, including electricity, railways, transportation and the post office. Circulation of goods and money ground to a halt. Republics competed for outside investment, fragmenting the market for foreign companies wishing to do business there. Tito recognised the threat to the future survival of Yugoslavia, but did nothing to combat the disintegration. Foreign borrowing during the 1970s shored the crumbling structure up for a while, but debts must be paid eventually.

After Tito's death in 1980, rumblings of discontent began again in Kosovo, when the Albanian majority began to press for independence from Serbian rule. They were brutally suppressed, and military rule, in the form of 100 tanks and 15,000 soldiers, was imposed. This is still in force and the Albanians are much oppressed. But Serbian fears of the Albanian majority had been aroused. Milosević rose to power largely through the backing of Kosovo Serbs, whose fears he exploited to his own ends.

The complex structure of committees and vetos which Tito set up to avoid any one person from replacing him was able to hold Yugoslavia together for a few years after Tito's death. But the fragmentation he introduced to deal with the nationalities issue was too far advanced to be stopped. When the collapse of Soviet communism removed the threat of armed intervention from the USSR, the disintegration of Tito's federation was swift and bloody.

As the end of Yugoslavia became ever more certain in 1991, Serb minorities in Croatia, Bosnia and Kosovo feared that they were about to be annihilated. In Croatia, many Serbs with high positions in the public service lost their jobs. There was a rumour that newspapers and magazines run by Serbs were to be banned. The police force was reorganised, replacing Serb officers with Croatian ones. Less educated people in the country areas believed that fascism was returning. The instant recognition accorded to Croatia by Germany reinforced this conviction, and added the spectre of a Fourth German Reich to the fears of the Serbs.

The declarations of Croatian and Slovenian independence set Yugoslavia aflame. The sequel has been described in Chapter 5. This is a war created by enduring hatreds from the past, reinforced by nationalism, religion and the cynical 'divide and rule' policies of Tito's Communists, and fostered today by ambitious and totally unscrupulous politicians who care nothing for the victims of their policies – whether these be their own people or others. The methods are those of the civil war – concentration camps, massacre, mutilation, torture and mass destruction. Under the horrible ethos of such wars – 'if you're not for us, you're against us' – people who were determined not to be sucked into unreasoning hatred of their neighbours and their friends have found themselves forced to choose sides. It is not uncommon for husband and wife of mixed marriages to be fighting on opposite sides.

Where will it end? The European Community and the United Nations have shown that they are incapable of effective action to stop the fighting. The arms embargo imposed by the international community has harmed only the Muslims, by denying them the materiel they must have to defend themselves, while the Serbs and Croats have had no difficulty obtaining fresh supplies. As a result, Muslim communities have been devastated, and some 30,000 to 50,000 women have become the victims of organised rape on a scale hitherto unknown. The Serbs have made enormous territorial gains.

It is hard to imagine that any permanent peace can ever be established now among the South Slavs. The future appears bleak indeed. The best that can be hoped for seems to be the partition of Bosnia and a massive relocation of peoples so that no sizeable minorities are left anywhere inside the new states' boundaries. The only alternative would be for all groups to agree on the same version of their collective history, accept its reality and immutability, and recognise that all have been as much sinned against as sinning in the past. Such a humane and rational solution to the tragedy seems at best unlikely.